Bill's Kitchen

Bill's Kitchen

I've spent my life making delicious simple food and that's what I want to share with you.

Bill Sewell

Photography by Jay Watson

archetype books

Contents

Introduction

Twenty years ago I wrote my last cookbook and all the time since then I've been unwittingly planning this new book. What has evolved is a collection of my very best recipes. They reflect my own particular food journey from meat-eating childhood to a decade of vegetarianism to an enthusiastically omnivorous present (for more on this food journey, see 'A Life of Food' on page 9).

This book is my equivalent of a singer's 'greatest hits'. These are the recipes which have stayed with me, my cafés and my family and friends.

For a dish to survive in the evolutionary jungle of café and home life, it needs two qualities. Firstly it needs to be reliably delicious – something you anticipate with excitement every time it's on offer. And secondly it needs to be simple to make.

At the cafés we have small kitchens and small kitchen teams. Recipes requiring fiddly culinary techniques don't work for us – and nor do they work for most domestic cooks. Many of our recipes have evolved at the cafés, but they are all designed for domestic cooking. None rely on fancy bits of kit. There are no water baths or dry ice: it's food for your kitchen, not for a lab. I'll admit in the privacy of these pages that I'm hopeless at spun sugar, filleting fish and all forms of fancy decoration. I would certainly never win Masterchef or Bake-off. But I've spent my life making delicious simple food and this book gives you the best of the best from my cooking life.

Some of these recipes are quick to make, some take longer, but they are all dependable and deliciously flavoursome, and the techniques are all simple. I'm excited by food that makes my mouth water – not simply because it's fashionable and cutting-edge.

Whilst all the recipes have been honed in my various kitchens, the ideas have come from all sorts of different places and people: from our many staff teams over nearly thirty years; from restaurants, pubs and cafés I've visited; from food writers, friends and family members. I always want to know the source of different recipes, so I always aim to credit the talented and generous people who have shared their knowledge and love of food.

Every cook has his or her own food journey and food story – and this is mine.

Grumpy Old

A life of food

My family tell me that I can turn a conversation on any subject to food in 20 seconds, and I like to think they're right. I see my life through the prism of food. With my morning granola, I'll be wondering where I can get some rabbit to cook with cider for supper; while I'm wolfing down jerk chicken at Café @ All Saints at lunchtime, I'll be thinking about trying out a new recipe for chocolate and cherry cake in the afternoon; and when planning our massed family summer holiday, I'm wondering if it's illegal to carry sourdough starter through customs.

When I'm reading a cookbook I'm always interested to know how recipes have arisen or arrived with the author, so I've written the mini food biography below for those of you who are similarly curious. If this life story stuff doesn't float your boat, then go straight to the recipes!

A small business childhood

My parents had an antique porcelain shop in Kensington Church St, London. During the week we lived above the shop with my grandmother ('Ti') who paid me with a spoonful of chunky marmalade to bring her morning newspaper upstairs each morning. Every Sunday evening she would give us three boys supper in her kitchen: Dairylea cheese triangles, those bizarre sliced luncheonmeat things with a perfect boiled egg running down the middle, and tinned guavas or mangoes to remind her of her time in India.

Mum was always busy combining working in the shop with looking after and cooking for us boys and my Dad. Her cooking would happen at the same time as washing the latest dinner service which Dad had bought, or pricing up the auction sale she was going to tomorrow. But she was a good proper cook; shepherd's pie, really good fry-ups, real beefburgers, home-made fishcakes, baked eggs. Puddings were basically variations on apple crumble, which might seem unimaginative but there's still a voice in me whispering that really good apple crumble is the only pudding worth having. When time was particularly pressing we would sometimes be given 50p to go to the Marina (subsequently re-named the Lago Blu and then, in a sign of changing times, taken over by Sally Clarke's wonderful eponymous restaurant in the late 1980s). The Marina was an old-fashioned British/Italian restaurant where in the early 1970s our 50p would buy us tuna fish salad and jam pancakes. If Mum and Dad came with us they would talk in code about auction prices (always believing that the next table, in this street of antique-dealers, was listening in). Very occasionally we were allowed zabaglione, properly made to order, a rich and exotic concoction that I still love but eat only very occasionally.

All our family holidays carry food memories for me. Camping holidays where Dad would proclaim his intention to give Mum a rest, and would make the one meal in his repertoire (a massive and delicious fry-up). This would arrive a couple of hours late to a starving family, and involved more stress and mess than Mum doing several meals of her own. Another camping holiday in France where we went to a restaurant and were served proper ratatouille – a dish of fragrant auberginey richness which bore no connection to the wet and sloppy vegetable stews which continue to bear the name of ratatouille to this day. Our one truly luxurious hotel holiday in Switzerland, where we were introduced to the joys of both meat fondue (rather pointless in my view – why not have a steak that's been cooked properly in the kitchen?) and cheese fondue (which I still think is utterly delicious right down to the crusty bit at the bottom of the pot).

There were three long summer holidays with my Scottish grandfather who lived in considerable style in upstate New York. Rina the cook made the most perfect rough chocolate chip cookies. I discovered where she kept the tin (and I think I've pretty much arrived at her recipe now – see page195). When this same grandfather and step grandmother came to stay in London (again in great style) we would get invited for a meal at the Connaught or whichever other grand London hotel they were staying in, and I could indulge in my childhood's perfect meal: avocado prawns; fillet steak; peach melba. I was a child of the seventies.

Saving the world by eating

As a teenager I continued to be a food enthusiast, but also developed a teenager's need to do good to the world (whether the world wanted it or not). My friend Ben and I wrote to our school magazine saying that the school should become vegetarian as that was a much more efficient way to use the world's resources. I wasn't yet a vegetarian at that stage, but after leaving school, a short spell working in the battery chicken operation of a kibbutz in Israel tipped me over the edge. And so I spent the next 10 years of my life completely immersed in the world of vegetarian cookery, and I continue to love great vegetarian food. It's a measure of the variety of non-meat cookery that of the 14 chapters of Harold McGee's *On Food and Cooking*, only one chapter is devoted to meat and meat cookery.

When I went to university at Trinity College Cambridge, I found that I enjoyed cooking more than history. Even more than the food itself, it was my friends' reactions to being cooked for that gradually lured me into a lifelong love of cooking. For me there were (and are) few things better than seeing the pleasure in peoples' faces enjoying a good meal that you've just made for them.

Every day when I'm at All Saints or Michaelhouse people will come up to me and say how much they've enjoyed their quiche or their Chelsea bun or their lamb tagine. The only job I've done outside the food business is being an accountant (a painful 4-year interlude in my twenties) and you certainly don't get people smilingly thanking you for a wonderful audit.

After Cambridge I immersed myself in the world of vegetarian cookery and vegetarian restaurants. My first cooking job was at Wilkins Natural Foods in Westminster. This was a classic 1980s vegetarian café, founded and run by an ex-Cranks manager, with a lot of hairy armpits on view and a strong line in Buddhism, brown pasta and gloopy sauces – but also a fantastic commitment to fresh, home-made food that has stayed with me ever since. There I learned to make bread and roll pastry, and began to appreciate both the differences and similarities between cooking at home and cooking on a bigger scale commercially.

After a short interlude as an accountant I then worked briefly at the (now Michelin-starred) Launceston Place in Kensington. They took me on as a veg-prep commis chef, but a couple of days after I started, their French pastry chef gave in his notice. I was given two days to learn his recipes and was then entrusted with the job of pastry chef there for the next couple of months. I learned to make tuile baskets, lemon tart, brandy snaps and ice cream. But more importantly I learned how a professional kitchen was organized – the insistence on consistent quality, discipline and cleanliness. It was a steep learning curve for me and a valuable experience. A world where Cambridge degrees and chartered accountancy qualifications counted for nothing, and you were only as good as your last service.

At the ripe old age of 25 I felt ready to create my own restaurant, and two years later opened The Place Below in the crypt of St Mary-le-Bow church in London. I wanted a restaurant where the food was all delicious – and just happened to be vegetarian. The ingredients at the heart of our menu were roast peppers and aubergines; our own bread; tons of fresh herbs; buffalo mozzarella, Parmesan and Beenleigh Blue; litres of olive oil and sacks of Puy lentils. But as much as the ingredients, it was the people who came and cooked at The Place Below who helped me develop our food. Ian Burleigh brought the ethics and commitment of traditional vegetarian cookery. Frances Tomlinson gave us the technical refinement of a Leith's training. We had chefs who had worked with Alistair Little at 192 and at Sally Clarke's. And just as importantly we had (as nearly all London restaurants did and still do) chefs from all over the world: Inez from Portugal who showed us what a proper Spanish omelette was like; Jurgen the anarchist German who made the most delicate oyster mushroom ravioli in saffron cream; Santi the Thai/Mexican who made superb Thai pancakes to serve with a crunchy spicy salad; and our Colombian kitchen porter who made illicit pineapple beer in a secret container under the sink.

The lure of the fleshpots

The 1980s were a great decade for cooking in London, and so also a great time for eating out. I had met Sarah just after The Place Below opened in 1989 and food

THE RIVER COTTAGE
MEAT
BOOK
Nigel Slater
COOKBOOK
GOOD HOUSEKEEPING
COOKERY BOOK

(at least from my perspective!) has always featured heavily in our relationship. Sarah was a barrister and so could afford to take us to restaurants that a young café owner couldn't reach. Perhaps not completely coincidentally, I stopped being a vegetarian shortly after we met (one too many plates of crudités was the straw that broke the camel's back) and this opened the way to an array of restaurants that would have held limited appeal to me in my vegetarian days. We ate pig's trotters at Pierre Koffmann's Tante Claire; the stunning Poulet en Vessie (Poulet de Bresse cooked in a pig's bladder with truffles under its skin and a pile of morels beside it) cooked by Joël Robuchon in Paris; delicious roast fennel at The River Café; fresh little ceps sautéed with cured ham at Laguiole; chocolate and rosemary pots at The Peat Inn. I could go on and on.

I've always felt that there is a seamless connection between great Michelin-starred cooking and great family and café cooking: it's all about honest ingredients, great flavours and taking care. The Mum cooking for her toddlers and Michel Roux at Le Gavroche both want to put a smile on the faces of their eaters.

Bringing bacon to the cafés

At my cafés I want to serve food that I find irresistibly delicious and so the café menus have always followed my own personal journey. I want to serve people what I want to eat. This is clearly not what a business consultant would advise, but then one of the pleasures of having your own business is that you don't always have to follow sensible advice.

The introduction of meat to the cafés has built over the last 15 years so that we now offer a fully omnivorous menu in both Hereford and Cambridge. I still love great vegetarian food and we still offer really excellent vegetarian dishes; but now I also love slow-cooked lamb, spicy roast chicken, sausage and onion-marmalade sandwiches, venison lasagne, rabbit and cider and beef and ale. And I want my customers to be able to enjoy all that too.

Family cooking

However, changing from being a vegetarian to a meat-eater is a minor shift compared with the change from life before children to life after children. And from a cooking and eating point of view that has been at least as big a journey.

Jonathan and Holly are 18 and 14 at the time of writing and are enthusiastic participants in gastronomic experiments. But it was not always thus. The scarring memories of strawberries that had to face the right way on the plate and meals redolent with threats and injunctions are still with me. And even though I actually like fish fingers and baked beans and pancakes I'm glad to have moved on to broader pastures now.

So whatever your personal food journey – and we are all on such a journey whether we're aware of it or not – I hope that my food will introduce you to some new tastes, build your confidence in some old favourites and contribute a few recipes which will eventually become old friends.

In this book I'm giving you my absolute favourite recipes from nearly 40 years of cooking and I hope you enjoy them. Happy cooking!

MODEL 1144
600g
MAX.5000g 0-5000g d=5g MAX.11lb 0-11lb d=0.2oz
ON
TARE
MODE
OFF

Measurements

Weights & volumes

In the recipe ingredient lists, weights and volumes are all metric. I always refer to proper cook's measuring spoons, and it's also useful to carry in your head the two basic sizes: 1 tsp = 5ml; 1 tbs = 15ml.

It's not always obvious whether to indicate the number of vegetables (e.g. 1 large potato) or the weight of the vegetable (e.g. 250g potato). I have used the one that I think will make the recipe easiest to follow; in some cases I give both versions, with the view that clarity is more important than consistency.

Tins: I've used net weights rather than drained weights, so a 400g tin of chickpeas means a tin with a net weight of 400g including the water/brine.

Fresh herbs: the supermarket that we most often shop in (the one with the orange bags) sells most herbs in 28g bunches; however, I refer to herbs by weight rather than by the bunch since if you're lucky enough to live near a good greengrocer or market you may buy your herbs in much larger bunches. When I specify 30g in a recipe, don't feel you have to go out and buy an extra bunch to make up the 2g difference (just in case the author of the most excellent *The Pedant in the Kitchen* is reading this)!

Salt: I've added specific salt measurements to many of the recipes, but do adjust as your tastebuds dictate.

Eggs: medium-size eggs unless specified otherwise.

Weights

Metric	Imperial
10g	½ oz
20g	¾ oz
25g	1 oz
40g	1½ oz
50g	2oz
60g	2½oz
75g	3oz
110g	4oz
125g	4½oz
150g	5oz
175g	6oz
200g	7oz
225g	8oz
250g	9oz
275g	10oz
350g	12oz
450g	1lb
700g	1½lb
900g	2lb
1.3kg	3lb

Volume

Metric	Imperial
55ml	2fl oz
75ml	3fl oz
150ml	5 fl oz
150ml	¼pint
275ml	10fl oz
275ml	½pint
425ml	15fl oz
425ml	¾pint
570ml	1pint
725ml	1¼pint
1 litre	1¾pint
1.2litre	2 pint
1.5litre	2½pint
2.25litre	4pint

1 tsp = 1 teaspoon (5ml)
1 dsp = 1 dessert spoon (10ml)
1 tbs = 1 tablespoon (15ml)

Weighing liquids for bread & measuring rice by volume

Traditionally liquids are measured in volume, and solids by weight. I'm increasingly finding that for bread-making it's easier and more accurate to weigh liquids. If you can, invest in a robust set of digital scales (see page 19). You can then put your bread-mixing bowl on the scales and weigh the flour, the sourdough starter and the water all in grams – much easier!

Conversely, when it comes to cooking rice, you want a basic volumetric ratio. For instance, for basmati rice, it's 1.5 times the volume of water to rice. The ratio is based on volume, so it makes sense to measure by volume.

If you get used to measuring liquids by weight rather than by volume it's worth knowing that, although 100ml of water weighs 100g, cooking oils such as olive oil are about 7% less dense than water, so if you want to weigh 100ml of olive oil, it weighs 93g (95g is fine if your digital scales measure in 5g increments).

Portion sizes

I like cooking generously – it's fundamental to how I feel about food, and my portions are on the large side. But equally, I don't want to over-feed people and I hate waste, so if you have a modest appetite and don't want leftovers, feel free to adapt quantities accordingly – apart from the cake and bread recipes, where the recipe quantities are best not tinkered with. Actually cooking with leftovers is probably my favourite kind of cooking (see pages 252-5 for more).

Oven temperatures

Unless otherwise specified I have used an electric fan oven and temperatures are given in centigrade (°C). To convert to a non-fan oven add 20 degrees °C. However, ovens vary considerably beyond this simple adjustment, and you may have to increase or reduce cooking times by as much as 25% , or adjust by up to 20 degrees. In the end you do have to use your eyes, nose and sense of touch to tell when things are cooked.

The need to use your senses applies even more strongly if you cook on Agas/Rayburns, whose temperatures do vary quite a bit. We each know our own Agas and you will need to adjust according to your experience.

In broad terms for a 4-cavity Aga:

Very hot oven 220°C – for bread/pizza – not reliably achievable on most Agas, but the floor or the top shelf of the top right oven are the hottest patches
Roasting oven 180/200°C – top right oven
Baking oven 150/160°C – bottom right oven
Simmering oven 110/120°C – top left oven
Plate warmer 50/60°C – bottom left oven

Fan °C	°C	Gas	°F
120	140	1	275
130	150	2	300
150	170	3	325
160	180	4	350
170	190	5	375
180	200	6	400
200	220	7	425
210	230	8	450
220	240	9	475

JUDGE
HOLD
ON/OFF

My favourite bits of kitchen equipment

This is not intended to be a list of everything you need for your first kitchen. This is a short list of my favourite extras. My guess is that most of you reading this have got most of the obvious essentials: we all need a good set of sharp knives, a stick blender, a reliable food processor, decent pans and a Le Creuset-type heavy-bottomed cast-iron casserole.

But here's my list of things which I love and make my kitchen life happier, and perhaps aren't on that obvious first list of kitchen essentials.

Robust digital scales

Digital temperature probe

Commercial clingfilm dispenser
No more fighting with clingfilm!

Stainless steel dough scraper and **plastic scraper**
For both cutting bread dough and pastries and cleaning work surfaces

Large non-stick frying pan with a lid
For stir-fries, finishing pasta, making sauces, making frittata and much else

At least two very light and large stainless steel mixing/salad bowls
No more struggling with tossing salads and mixing bread dough in bowls that are nearly (but not quite) big enough

Agas and other range cookers

I'm a late convert to traditional range cookers. I sneered for years at their wastefulness and uncontrollability. Then we moved into a house that had a generous and well organized Nobel (a now defunct brand that works just like an Aga) already installed and I've slowly realized how lovely they can be. We live in a large, poorly insulated house. The only room that we've managed to insulate properly is the kitchen and the Nobel keeps it utterly cosy even in fairly cold winters. Its well sealed oven is fantastic for slow-cooked meat dishes. Its always-on warming oven is great for keeping food warm without having to think of turning the oven on low. The top is great for keeping cups of tea warm, leaning against when cold and drying laundry and wet trainers. None of these things take away the wastefulness and uncontrollability, but there are hugely seductive compensating benefits so long as you have a decent normal oven nearby as well!

However, in order that the cooking instructions in this book should be universal I've given them in standard temperatures. Many recipes will happily convert to hot and medium Aga equivalents and if you're an Aga aficionado you won't need me to provide instruction. However, I'd always prefer to make bread and cakes in a standard oven.

Bread: daily & less daily

Good bread gives me more pleasure than almost any other food. Both making and eating bread makes me happy. Even buying good bread from proper artisan bakeries is a pleasure, whether it's a traditional family-run bakery in France or a hipster start-up in Bristol. In proper bakeries we're given the sight of great troughs of dough being kneaded, the smell of freshly baked loaves being pulled from the oven, and the taste and texture of real food. So it's a mystery to me why so many people so regularly choose to ignore a cheap and daily pleasure of the senses. Maybe we can't all make our own bread all the time – but let's eat only good bread made either at home or at a decent bakery, café or restaurant. Let's choose pleasure over dullness!

It's always been central to my cafés that we make our own bread each day, but both our café bread-making and mine at home has evolved over time. Our doughs are now wetter, slower-proving and in some cases feature sourdough starter – also known as leaven or natural yeast. Wetter doughs make a moister crumb and a crisper crust. Together with slower proving and briefer but more frequent kneading, these wetter doughs produce a massively improved crumb structure – more chewy and less crumbly. And the addition of sourdough – whilst not everyone's cup of tea – for me adds a transformative depth of flavour achievable in no other way.

My bread journey has been guided and inspired by many unstinting and experienced bakers. My thanks to all of you. Unsurprisingly sourdough baking is also a subject that has generated a vast number of discussion groups and blogs on the web, many of which are generous and helpful.

I realise that many of you reading this may lead a sad existence without a reassuring pot of sourdough starter in your fridge waiting to be used, so all the recipes in this chapter (except the simple white sourdough loaf) include non-sourdough alternatives. But I'd encourage you to start on the sourdough adventure – see page 26 for more.

Even if you already make and love the breads from my original cookbooks, I urge you to try these new recipes. As well as the daily breads, there are some delicious but probably more occasional treats – buttery brioche, sticky Chelsea buns and cheese and tomato buns.

Bill's wholemeal loaf

The method for this updated version of our daily bread is adapted from Dan Lepard's *The Handmade Loaf*. The theory is that the bran in wholemeal flour is sharp and cuts through the gluten of the dough if you knead it too much. So most of the bread's structure is formed by letting it sit between rather brief sessions of kneading. Don't worry too much about the precise timing given below – the point is to knead a small amount and let the dough rest in between. It's deliciously dense and moist with a very good crust – and like most bread it freezes very well.

At the cafés we use a bit of sourdough starter, but it's not essential, and a non-sourdough alternative is given here.

It's rather a wet dough with a tendency to spread, so once it rises more than a couple of cm above the edge of the tin, it might create muffin tops (i.e. sag over the edge). You'll need to stick it in the oven just before this point.

Makes 1 large loaf (2lb/1kg tin) or 2 small (1lb/500g tins)

425g lukewarm water

50g orange juice

100g sourdough starter (if not using sourdough starter add an additional 50g wholemeal flour and 50g lukewarm water)

475g strong wholemeal flour

100g strong white flour

25g sunflower seeds

25g sesame seeds

10g salt

7g instant yeast (1 sachet)

Put all the ingredients (wet ingredients first) into a large bowl and mix until the ingredients are all combined – I use a large metal spoon for this. You should do no kneading at this point.

Leave for 5 minutes, then knead very briefly – just a couple of good stretches of the dough. Leave for another 5 minutes, then knead very briefly.

Leave for a third lot of 5 minutes, then knead briefly.

Leave for 10 minutes, then it's ready to go into the tins.

Tip the dough onto a work surface and weigh out the correct number of pieces (1.2kg for large loaves, 600g for small ones). Shape the dough so that all the creases are on the underside and then put into oiled tins. The dough should be an even sausage, if anything slightly thicker at the ends than in the middle, to make a loaf that is as even as possible rather than domed in the centre.

Leave to prove in a warm place for 45-90 minutes (until about 2cm above the height of the tins).

Pre-heat the oven to 220°C (fan). Bake for 40 minutes (30 minutes for smaller loaves) until the loaf or loaves are well browned. Take out of the oven, remove from the tin, and tap the bottom of each loaf – if it doesn't sound hollow, bake for a bit longer. Once it's cooked and out of the tin, leave to cool on wire racks.

Ciabatta rolls & loaves

At the cafés we use this dough to make our pizza bases, rolls and baps, and it also makes great ciabatta loaves. As with our brown loaves, we use a mixture of sourdough starter and normal dried yeast, to combine depth of flavour with a normal rise. But you can also use ordinary instant yeast on its own, as in the recipe below.

Once the dough has risen in bulk, you want to preserve the structure by being gentle with your shaping. Wetter bread doughs takes a bit of getting used to – a proper dough scraper (see page 19) will make your life easier. You'll need extra flour to shape the baps and rolls, and a little more to sprinkle on the baps after they are baked.

Makes 1kg of dough – enough for 7 large baps, or 15 smaller rolls, or a large loaf and a few small rolls, or 6 x 160g pizza bases (see page 221 for more on pizza creation).

The night before

200g cold water

50g sourdough starter

(if you've no sourdough starter then add an additional 50g flour and 50g water and 7g sachet dried yeast)

200g strong white flour

The next morning

350g strong white flour

175g warm water

30g olive oil

7g sachet dried yeast

10g salt

The night before

Mix all the 'night before' ingredients together until you've got a smooth mix, then cover with a lid/clingfilm and leave at room temperature overnight. This mixture is known as a 'sponge'.

The next morning

Add the rest of the ingredients to the overnight sponge and knead with a dough hook or by hand until you have a smooth mix. This should not take longer than a couple of minutes. Leave to prove in bulk for an hour or so in a warm place until roughly doubled in size and then pour onto a lightly floured workbench.

Shape the rolls. Our cafés use 140g baps for sandwiches, 60g rolls to go with soup and an in-between-sized oval roll for Tudge's bacon and sausage baps. Cut the dough into 2 fat sausages, using a lightly floured dough scraper. Cut the sausage into the desired sizes. You can bake them as they are, or you can gently shape them by hand so they are roughly uniform. If you're making loaves, simply cut the dough into three slipper-shaped sausages – 'ciabatta' means slipper. Then use the dough scraper to transfer the rolls/loaves to baking sheets lined with baking parchment (the dough has a tendency to stick to the baking sheets without the parchment).

Prove it all in a warm place for about 30-50 minutes until it's all puffy and risen. Bake the rolls for 14 mins at 220°C (fan). For ciabatta loaves bake at 220°C (fan) for about 20 minutes until browning and hollow sounding when tapped on the bottom.

Making & nurturing a sourdough starter

Sourdough breads are made using a natural leaven in place of either fresh or dried yeast. A mixture of flour and water (and sometimes additional yeast-friendly things such as grapeskins, raisins or yoghurt) is left at room temperature where it attracts and becomes a feeding-ground for yeasts and bacteria which naturally occur in the air everywhere. This mixture is then fed in a controlled way to promote the growth and activity of these natural yeasts and bacteria until you have a fully developed and lively starter.

Although many sourdough recipes suggest feeding your starter (once it's established) with equal weights of water and flour, I've found that a slightly higher proportion of flour, including a small amount of rye flour, improves the taste of the bread.

If you've never dealt with sourdough before, the easiest way to begin is to beg, borrow or steal from a friend, or from one of our cafés. But if neither of those strategies works for you then here's how to start from scratch.

Starting a starter

These instructions are adapted from Dan Lepard's *The Handmade Loaf.*

I usually establish a routine so that I feed my sourdough at roughly the same time each day. Throughout this process you should keep your starter at room temperature, i.e. around 20°C, to keep it lively. Once you've got a bit of starter you need to either feed it daily at room temperature, or put it in the fridge to preserve it for future use; for instance if you're not going to use it for a few days/weeks/months.

Nurturing your starter

If you're making bread daily then it's an easy and routine process as you simply feed your starter just after you've made your bread. If you're just making an occasional or weekly batch then it's slightly more complicated. The sourdough starter will keep happily in the fridge for weeks but if it's been there for more than a week then you want to give it 3 days of being fed daily at room temperature (see 'Day 5' on page 27) before making a loaf with it. It is remarkable how an unattractive pot of sludge covered in brownish liquid will return to beautiful lively starter with three days of being fed at room temperature.

If you've only left the starter in the fridge for a couple of days then it will probably only need one day's feeding to bring it back to full liveliness. If you're making bread once a week, as many home bakers do, you can either feed and discard every day at room temperature (which feels a bit wasteful), or if you were, say, baking at the weekend, you could prepare your dough for baking, then feed your remaining starter and put it in the fridge. If you then take it out of the fridge on Friday and feed it and leave at room temperature, it should be ready for dough-making by Saturday afternoon. A creamy bubbly look and a (to me) delicious yoghurty aroma are the signs of a lively starter that's ready to use. Use your eyes and nose – it may need another day of feeding to bring it back to full life.

To test if your starter is lively and ready to use, add a bit to some water. If it's ready it will float on the surface, not so thin that it just dissolves, or so heavy that it sinks.

Day 1

40g water at room temperature

2 tsp rye flour

2 tsp strong white flour

2 tsp raisins

I optional tbs plain live yoghurt

Day 2

40g water at room temperature

2 tsp rye flour

2 tsp strong white flour

Day 3

80g water at room temperature

4 tsp strong white flour

4 tsp rye flour

Day 4

100g water at room temperature

25g rye flour

100g strong white flour

Day 5

100g water at room temperature

25g rye flour

100g strong white flour

For the first 3 days

You'll need to use a large jam jar or kilner jar. Each day, you add in the day's ingredients, mix well, and leave with the lid on.

The mixture will slowly alter in appearance, as it works towards fermentation.

Day 4

By now some bubbles/froth of fermentation should appear. Discard about threequarters of the mixture. You can strain the remainder to get rid of the raisins, but I've never bothered, and they seem to disappear very soon. Add Day 4's flour and water to the mixture, stir well and leave with the lid on.

Day 5

If you've been given 100g of starter this is the point at which you join the process.

When you open the lid you should smell a yoghurty smell and the mixture should look somewhat bubbly. Discard threequarters of it, add the water and flour and mix well to form a thick paste. Leave with the lid on.

You now just repeat Day 5 for ever more. If you're just maintaining the starter, then discard threequarters as usual. If you want to make some bread, use some of the mixture you're about to discard (about 200g starter for 1 large loaf, see page 29) as the basis for your bread. If you want to make larger quantities of bread then use a bit more of the mixture that's due to be discarded, and double the quantity of flour/water that you add to it. Whether making bread or not, add water and flour to the remaining mixture as usual, mix well and leave with the lid on.

Simple white sourdough loaf

Most professional craft bakers prove sourdough loaves in special baskets ('bannetons') and then transfer them direct to the oven floor. However, I'm a recovering accountant and I like these loaves orderly and loaf-shaped, which is both easier and creates the right-shaped slices for sandwiches and toast.

This is a stunningly good everyday loaf with a delicious flavour and a wonderful chewy texture. Note that it proves overnight – either in the fridge or in a cool room. We have a larder at home which tends to be around 15°C, perfect for overnight proving of this loaf. But in our cafés, where the kitchens are generally much warmer, the loaves would overprove if we left them out of the fridge overnight. A lot of variables will affect how quickly your loaves rise: the temperature of the dough when it goes into the tins, the liveliness of the starter, the temperature of the fridge; in the end you need to assess by eye when the loaf is ready to bake.

Makes 1 x 900g loaf or 2 x 450g loaves

Use one 2lb/1kg loaf tin for a large loaf, or two 1lb/500g tins for two small loaves

200g sourdough starter (page 26)

275g lukewarm water

450g strong white flour

5g salt

Mix everything together thoroughly, using either a food mixer with a dough hook or a large spoon. Leave in the mixing bowl for 30 mins at room temperature and then knead briefly. With this bread I find it creates less mess to do the kneading within the same bowl – otherwise you're constantly cleaning your work surface (if you're using a mixer with a dough hook then just leave the dough in the mixing bowl throughout). Leave for one more hour at room temperature, then knead again briefly.

Oil the tins. Weigh the dough out to the correct sized blobs, and shape it into fat sausages the length of the tins. Put in the tins and leave to prove overnight, either in a cool room or in the fridge. By the morning the dough may be bulging promisingly above the top of the tins (but this will depend on the temperature of your kitchen or your fridge as well as the liveliness of your starter). If the loaves have not risen enough, take them out of the fridge and continue to prove for between 1-4 hours in a warm place, until they have risen at least 2cm above the top of the tin. Be patient – the whole experience will be very disappointing if you bake the loaves before they've sufficiently risen.

Bake at 220°C (fan) for 35 mins (25 minutes for the smaller loaves) until a deep golden brown on the outside and hollow-sounding when tapped on the bottom of the loaf.

Try to be patient one last time and allow to cool before eating.

Spianata

This is based on an Italian bread from Romagna which I came across at a superb London sandwich bar (also called Spianata) where they bake it fresh each morning. At the time of writing this is my favourite bread.

Spianare means to 'level' or 'roll out'. This dough is so liquid it's almost more like a batter than a dough. You start with an overnight 'sponge' and then add flour, water, more yeast, and salt the next morning. It's typically made in quite large sheets, but at home it's easier to make smaller sheets of roughly the same total area. These quantities are designed for 2 tins measuring about 280mm x 320mm, about 20mm deep – or the equivalent.

I give both sourdough and instant yeast versions of this recipe below. Both versions have a delightfully uneven and chewy interior with large bubbles – superb for mopping up gravy juices or making a perfect cheese sandwich.

The night before

450g strong white flour (400g if using sourdough)

450g cold water (400g if using sourdough)

7g sachet instant yeast (or substitute 100g sourdough starter)

The next morning

600g strong white flour

425g warm water

7g sachet instant yeast (omit this if you've used sourdough)

25g salt

25ml olive oil (approx.) to go on top of the loaf – not for mixing in with the dough

The night before

Mix the 'night before' ingredients together until you've got a smooth mix. Cover with clingfilm and leave at room temperature overnight.

The next morning

Add the 'next morning' ingredients, except for the olive oil, to the overnight mix and knead with a couple of large metal spoons or with one hand for 1-2 minutes until you have a smooth mix. It's very unlike kneading a traditional dough as it's so wet and sticky.

Leave to rise until bubbly and roughly doubled in size – about 45 minutes (3-4 hours if using sourdough).

Line your tins with baking parchment or re-usable baking liner, and pour/scrape the dough into the tins.

Drizzle the olive oil over the top of the dough and put a bit more on your hands. Then use both hands to spread the dough gently and evenly over the tray right to the edges – it should be only very roughly level. Leave to prove in a warm place for about 30 minutes if using ordinary yeast, or an hour if using sourdough, until it looks bubbly and puffy. Pre-heat the oven to 220°C (fan).

Bake for 18 minutes until golden on top. Turn out onto a wire rack to cool. Once cooled (a bit) it's ready to cut into squares and slice horizontally for sandwiches.

Chelsea buns

Sticky, rich and delicious, these Chelsea buns are the best! And if you foolishly don't eat them all straight away, even several days later a few seconds in the microwave will bring them back to a highly acceptable aromatic warmth. I started off with the recipe in Linda Collister's excellent *Bread Book*, and from there I've developed a cinnamon-flavoured bun that is delicious and extremely moreish. We now make these in the cafés every day.

They aren't difficult to make but they do take a bit of time. Choose a cold winter weekend when there are good things on the radio, and don't rush it. I use a silicone cake mould which is 22cm square. It's fairly crucial that the tin you use has roughly these dimensions (or a similar total area) as the buns need to fit in snugly.

Makes 9 buns

For the dough

450g strong white flour

5g salt

40g caster sugar

7g sachet dried yeast

210g milk

60g butter, melted

1 egg, beaten

For the filling

40g butter, melted

100g light muscovado sugar

200g raisins

5g ground cinnamon (about 1 dsp)

For the glaze

50g honey

90g butter

120g light muscovado sugar

Grease your tin/silicone mould and line with greaseproof paper.

Put all the dough ingredients in a food mixer and knead with the dough hook for about 5 minutes. Cover the bowl with clingfilm and leave to rise for 1-2 hours until roughly doubled in size.

Roll the dough out to a rectangle measuring about 25cm x 40cm. For the filling, mix together the butter, sugar, raisins and cinnamon and spread over the rectangle of dough leaving a margin of about 1cm at the far edge. Then roll it up like a Swiss roll as tightly as possible, starting at the near long edge and finishing with the seam at the bottom.

Divide the roll into 9 pieces with a dough cutter and put each of them cut side uppermost into the tin, quite close together but barely touching. Leave to rise until at least doubled in size. This can take 1 to 2 hours depending on the temperature of the kitchen.

In a small pan stir all the glaze ingredients together. Once the buns have at least doubled in size, pour half the glaze over and bake at 180°C (fan) for 25-30 minutes, until the buns are golden brown and the dough in the middle springs back to the touch. When they come out of the oven, brush with the remainder of the glaze. Allow to cool for at least 10 minutes before serving.

It's best to serve the buns straight from the container you've baked them in or you'll lose valuable sticky goo in transit. These are most delicious when still warm.

Cheese & tomato buns; cheese & bacon buns

These buns are halfway between a rolled-up pizza and a savoury Chelsea bun, and they are especially delicious when still slightly warm.

As with all recipes the quality of ingredients is crucial – really well flavoured cheddar and proper dry-cured smoked bacon will make all the difference. I suspect that this approach would work well with other fillings (such as Gruyère and mushroom, or roast squash and Stilton) – give them a try and let me know!

These rolls are also very good made with the ciabatta dough on page 25. I've also made mini versions to serve warm with a glass of bubbly as a pre-dinner nibble – very delicious.

Makes 16 buns altogether

For the dough

700g strong white flour

20g salt

7g sachet instant yeast

450ml tepid water

70ml olive oil

For the filling – 8 of each flavour

75g sun-dried tomatoes in oil, whizzed

½ clove garlic, crushed

200g grated mature cheddar (half for each type of bun)

125g good quality smoked streaky bacon, diced 2cm, fried until crisp – retain the fat.

Mix all the dough ingredients together and knead for about 5 minutes until you have a smooth and elastic dough – either by hand or with a mixer using a dough hook. Once kneaded, cover the mixing bowl with clingfilm and leave to rise in a warm place for about an hour, until roughly doubled in size.

Cut the dough in half and roll each half out to a rectangle about 40cm x 30cm, with the long side towards you.

For the cheese and tomato buns, spread the whizzed-up tomato and the crushed garlic on the first rectangle, leaving a 2cm border at the end away from you. Then sprinkle half the cheese over. Roll up as tightly as you are able and cut into eight slices.

For the cheese and bacon buns, spread the crisp bacon bits, and any of the fat that has cooked out of the bacon, over the second rectangle leaving a 2cm border at the end away from you. Then sprinkle the rest of the cheese over. Roll up as tightly as you are able and then slice into eight.

Place on baking parchment on a baking tray, cut side facing up, and squish each bun briefly but firmly downwards with the palm of your hand. Leave to prove in a warm place for 30-60 minutes until at least doubled in size.

Bake at 220°C (fan) for about 12 minutes until beginning to brown. The buns should sound hollow when tapped on the bottom. Leave to cool on a wire rack until you can't resist them any longer.

Brioche

Proper home-made brioche is something quite special. Ideally you should eat it on its own or with home-made jam, but it also has numerous savoury uses. Try a glass of Sauternes with toasted slices of brioche and some rich liver paté such as foie gras. Or see the leek and Gruyère brioche recipe on page 177. And any spare brioche which you're foolish enough to let go stale makes exceptionally fine bread and butter pudding (see page 255).

You can use a proper fluted brioche mould for the big brioche but either a 500g loaf tin or free-formed loaves are also good. Kneading this dough by hand is very hard work so I'm only giving instructions for using a mixer.

Makes 1 large brioche and 4 little ones or 12 burger buns or small brioches

400g strong white flour

4 eggs

60ml milk, tepid

5g salt

25g sugar

7g sachet instant yeast

200g butter, softened

For glazing

1 egg yolk

pinch of salt

1 tbs water

Start the day before you want to bake the brioche. In the mixer bowl put everything except the butter and the glazing ingredients. Mix briefly with a wooden spoon to get it all started, then with the dough hook knead for about 5 minutes until the mixture is smooth.

Add the butter a quarter at a time, kneading for about 1 minute after each addition. If the dough hook doesn't reach quite to the sides of the bowl you may need to stop it from time to time and scrape the dough back into the middle. You should end up with a glossy smooth mixture. Cover with clingfilm and leave to rise for 1-2 hours until roughly doubled in size. Knock back, cover again and put in the fridge overnight.

Next day shape the brioche. Divide the dough: 600g for the big brioche and the rest divided in four (about 75g each) for the little ones or burger buns. If you're using a traditional brioche tin, lightly butter it. Divide the big bit of dough 200g/400g. Shape the larger part into a sphere and put this in the tin. With your fingers make a hole in the middle of it, shape a small oblong with the smaller bit of dough and put this in the hole. Then put the little brioches either in traditional mini brioche moulds (following the same procedure as for the big one) or (much easier) into muffin cases in muffin tins.

Leave it all in a properly warm place for 2-3 hours until slightly more than doubled in size. Pre-heat the oven to 180°C (fan). Glaze the brioches with egg yolk mixed with the water and salt. Bake the small ones for 14 minutes and the big one for 30 minutes until they are a dark golden brown and sound hollow when tapped on the bottom. Cool on a wire rack.

Holiday breakfasts

Nothing says holiday quite as engagingly as breakfast. The day starts late after a glass of wine the night before. People drift downstairs in dressing gowns or dinosaur-style onesies. There's time for a long, slow first cup of tea and then a pause to think about what shape breakfast will take. Different holidays for me mean different kinds of breakfast.

Big family holidays in Italy or France mean ripe tomatoes, melon, prosciutto and local cheese all with home-made flatbread. One of our family favourites is sliced Italian tomatoes drizzled with olive oil, particularly delicious on toasted Tuscan bread or spianata, which we rub with a garlic clove. Add some basil leaves and some shavings of Parmesan or Pecorino. Simple but perfect.

Weekend breakfasts with the cousins in Yorkshire may mean pancakes and coffee, while Saturday breakfasts at home currently mean Parkrun followed by a classic fry-up with Pomiane tomatoes or possibly (for me) a variation on Huevos Rancheros. Sundays suggest freshly baked brioche (in the bread chapter on page 37) with home-made blackcurrant jam – but only if I've got up early enough. And when school holidays come round my cafés will have a run on eggy bread with maple syrup and bacon.

But even normal weekdays can feel like holidays at breakfast time. It's a moment of the day which always feels special, and so I've also given here the recipe for our utterly superb granola, which we serve at the cafés every day and is also my daily treat at home – with comice pears, plums or raspberries and (full-fat) ginger yoghurt.

Relax and enjoy…

Granola

You can buy quite good granola but even the best bought granola isn't a patch on this home-made version. The ingredients here are more generous, the toasting is darker and it's inevitably fresher. We always have it on the menu at All Saints and we usually have a batch on the go at home as well.

This recipe is adapted from Nigella Lawson who got it from a café in Connecticut, New England. I think it's best when it is toasted quite brown – certainly darker than, say, Jordan's Crunchy. You can vary this recipe in any number of ways: more/less fruit, more/less nuts, but I think this version gives a really good balance for a daily feast. It's worth getting better quality larger oats for this. Sainsbury's sell a brand called Flahavan's that works very well.

If you're looking to make it all sweeter and richer I've discovered that it's stunningly good with some salted caramel walnut crumb (see page 209) stirred in. I probably wouldn't want this every day, but just occasionally it's lovely. Marianne, my editor, suggests you try it with ground coriander or nutmeg, for something more exotic.

Serve with 2 dsps Greek yoghurt and perhaps some fresh berries or fruit compote.

Makes enough for about 20 modest breakfasts

For this quantity you need 2 large baking trays (e.g. 28cm x 32cm) – alternatively you can make half the quantity

500g rolled oats

150g sunflower seeds

150g sesame seeds

150g flaked almonds

150g golden syrup

75g runny honey (melt first if using set honey)

½ tsp salt

2 tbs sunflower oil

300g raisins

Mix everything together thoroughly except the raisins. Mixing is an under-rated kitchen skill. Thorough mixing makes a real difference to this. If you have a Kenwood Chef or similar this makes the mixing much easier. Divide between your 2 large baking trays.

Bake at 150°C (fan) for about 45 minutes in total. Take it out after every 15 minutes and turn it over thoroughly so it gets evenly browned.

Take out of the oven and cool to room temperature. Mix in the raisins. Store in an airtight box until needed.

Bircher muesli

Dishes which are enduring national classics generally endure for good reasons: roast beef and Yorkshire pudding, rice and dahl, fondue Savoyarde, the list could go on and on. So it's no surprise to me that a classic Swiss bircher muesli is so delicious. We've served this for many years, first in London and now in Cambridge, and I never get bored of it. For me it's crucial that it should be on the sloppy side – better add too much apple juice than too little.

Toasting the hazelnuts is not essential but it is nice. I prefer nuts fairly small but not like powder. I like this both the moment it's been made and on subsequent days – it will keep up to a week in the fridge. The oats will become a bit more 'soaked', and the dish less textured, as time goes by. Both stages are good.

It's pretty and delicious garnished with fresh berries or ripe mango.

Serves 8

250g rolled oats

150g hazelnuts, toasted and roughly chopped in a food processor

750ml good quality apple juice

60g runny honey (melt first if using set honey)

750g Greek yoghurt – proper full fat stuff

500g eating apples, cored and grated

Mix everything together and check to see if the sweetness is about right for you. Add additional honey or apple juice to taste. Eat.

And if there's any left over, put it in the fridge till you want it.

Holiday fry-up with almost-Pomiane tomatoes

I'm a devoted granola man for everyday breakfasts (see page 41) but there is nothing that says 'holiday' to me so clearly as a proper cooked breakfast. Some of my family sometimes manage the Saturday Parkrun. When we do, it's obviously important to replace any lost calories as soon as possible, so this is what we have afterwards. The essentials of a post-Parkrun cooked breakfast are softly scrambled eggs on our brown toast, good smoked bacon, fried mushrooms and almost-Pomiane tomatoes. Tudge's sausages are a very acceptable extra.

Doing cooked breakfast for lots of people can be quite stressy and the way to avoid the stress is to have somewhere to keep plates, bacon (sausages if you're having them) and mushrooms warm whilst the tomatoes (which take the longest) finish cooking and you cook (at the last minute) the toast and scrambled eggs. I'm not giving recipes for cooking bacon, eggs or mushrooms – but here's the lowdown on these very delicious tomatoes.

The original recipe by Edouard de Pomiane (Tomates a la crème) has some double cream added at the end but for me that's too rich on top of the butter as well as the scrambled eggs and bacon and butter-fried mushrooms. This is so simple that it's barely a recipe, but it is stunningly good, even when made with wintery not very ripe tomatoes.

Serves 4

35g butter

4 medium tomatoes, halved – plum tomatoes are perfect

salt and pepper

Heat the butter in a small frying pan. When it's foaming add the tomatoes skin-side down. Cook on a medium heat for about 7 minutes, then season with salt and pepper and turn them over. Cook for another couple of minutes, then push them down slightly to release their liquid and turn down the heat. Cook for a further 5-10 minutes until they are completely soft and surrounded by a buttery tomatoey juice. Serve.

Egg poached in tomato & chorizo

Huevos not quite rancheros

This is along the lines of Huevos Rancheros but is ultra simple to make – which is a good thing at breakfast time when your concentration and energy levels may be modest. The dish is started on the hob and then the poaching of the egg finished in the oven. This works fine if you've got an Aga that is on anyway. If you haven't and you feel that it's a waste to switch your oven on just to poach an egg, then you can put a lid on the pan and finish the poaching on the hob – it doesn't seem to turn out quite as pretty that way but it tastes just the same.

The quality of the toast (such as the toasted ciabatta pictured here) makes all the difference to this dish.

Serves 1

1 tbs olive oil

1 cooking chorizo, halved lengthways and then cut 2cm

1 large tomato, diced 2cm

1 big egg

2 good slices very good toast – e.g. white sourdough, spianata, ciabatta or Bill's loaf

Pre-heat the oven to 160°C (fan).

Use a very small frying pan that can go into the oven or, ideally, a small cast-iron pan like the one pictured. Fry the chunks of chorizo in the olive oil for about 5 minutes until just cooked. Add the chopped tomato and fry for three or four minutes until the tomato is going mushy. Make a dip in the middle of the pan and crack the egg into the middle of this dip. Put in the oven for about 5 minutes until the white is just set and the yolk is still runny. Serve on a warmed plate with very good toast on the side.

The right sort of pancakes

These are proper thin pancakes, not the fluffy kind which I find less delightful.

For pancake fillings/toppings, bacon and maple syrup or ham and cheese are joyous, but it's hard to beat lemon juice and sugar. With these, try melting a little knob of butter on each one after you've flipped it. If cheese is one of your toppings, add it after the first flip so it begins to melt whilst the pancake is still in the pan.

Over 20 years ago I bought two cast-iron, flat-bottomed pancake pans and they have served me well ever since. I only ever use them for pancakes and when I've finished cooking I just wipe out any burnt bits and give them a very thin coating of sunflower oil and put them away.

Makes about 12 pancakes using a 20cm diameter pan

Batter

125g plain flour

pinch of salt

1 egg

330ml milk

Sunflower oil for frying

Choice of toppings

streaky bacon, cooked

smoked ham, thinly sliced

Gruyère or cheddar cheese, grated

lemon wedges

caster sugar

maple syrup

butter

good jam

Put all the batter ingredients in a large jug and whizz with a stick blender for 30 seconds until you have a smooth batter about the thickness of single cream. Leave to stand for half an hour.

Prepare your toppings before you start to cook the pancakes. Fry the bacon and keep it warm. Grate the cheese and have sliced ham ready to use. Have wedges of lemon ready and a bowl of sugar to go with it. Open a pot of blackcurrant jam.

When your toppings are ready, smear a little sunflower oil all over the bottom of your pancake pan with kitchen paper and heat it until it's very hot, so that a bit of batter dropped in starts to sizzle straight away. Put in a ladleful (I use about 60ml per pancake) and swirl it around quickly so that it covers the whole of the base of the pan. Let it cook for 30 seconds to a minute and then use a metal palette knife to ease it away from the pan all around the edge – you'll be able to see if it's cooked on the first side or not. When it's ready flip it over – I use a palette knife to do this but you may wish to toss it in the air – and cook very briefly on the other side until just beginning to brown. Serve immediately, with your toppings, or stack the pancakes in a warm place until you're ready to eat.

Of course the other thing that goes beautifully with bacon and maple syrup is eggy bread. Just soak a thickish piece of bread in an egg lightly beaten with a splash of milk and then fry it in a mixture of butter and sunflower oil until golden brown on both sides.

My favourite soups

There are basically three kinds of soup in my world: the first is the rich and creamy type often featuring winter vegetables; then there is soup 'with bits in', i.e. minestrone-type soups which for me include pulses of some kind. Thirdly, there are soups using meat stocks made from leftovers. In all three styles I'm looking for strong flavours, winter vigour and warmth.

For the rich and creamy blended soups, the key to deliciousness is sweating the vegetables with plenty of fat (olive oil/butter/sunflower oil) and some salt for long enough to make them really tender. Cooking with salt at this stage helps to pull water out of the vegetables and softens them more quickly. The final blended soup will then be deliciously smooth. There is of course a whole world of other wonderful puréed soups – curried parsnip, celeriac and Stilton, leek and potato etc – but the two given here provide a delicious starting point.

For the minestrone-type soups the key is to build sufficient flavour in the broth. This is what will make or break the soup. It's a bit like making gravy: there's a whole palette of ingredients, and the skill is in creating the right balance between sweetness, acidity, saltiness and spiciness. The list of potential ingredients used to create this balance might include wine, soy sauce, tomatoes, lemon juice, ginger, garlic, chillies, tamarind and other spices, herbs (both dried and fresh) sugar, coconut milk and, of course, salt. The three 'with bits in' recipes here give you some ready-made answers, but the pleasure of creating your own soup is in building a broth that tickles your particular tastebuds. Some recipes (cakes and bread particularly) are to be followed religiously; others are intended as starting points for exploration. Minestrone-type soups very much fall into the latter category.

It's worth being aware that soups using pulses almost always require a bit more acidity than you might expect – hence the presence of tomatoes, vinegar and tamarind in these recipes.

Finally there are soups that make use of leftover chicken carcasses and ham stock. For some brief words about chicken and sweetcorn soup and ham and pea soup, see page 63.

Parsnip, cheddar & rosemary soup

A rich, smooth, creamy, winter soup, given piquancy by the rosemary, mustard and cheese.

What makes this soup really good is the generous amount of butter and olive oil used to sweat the vegetables and the length of time the vegetables are sweated for. The parsnips should be completely soft before any liquid is added.

Serves 6

75g butter

30ml olive oil

175g onion (1 medium one), roughly chopped

3 sticks celery, roughly chopped

500g parsnips, peeled and sliced in 1cm rounds

2 cloves garlic, crushed

1 tsp salt

1 dsp chopped fresh rosemary

1 litre water

350g potatoes, peeled and chopped in 2cm pieces

2 tsp English mustard

150g strong cheddar, grated

seasoning

Melt the butter and olive oil in a large pan. Add the onion, celery, parsnips, garlic, salt and rosemary, stir well, and then cook on a low heat with the lid on for about 25 minutes until the parsnips are very soft but not browned. Give the vegetables a good stir every few minutes so that they don't stick and burn.

Add the water and potatoes and bring to the boil. Turn down the heat and continue simmering for about 25 minutes until the potatoes are completely soft and just starting to disintegrate.

Take off the heat and stir in the mustard. Purée the soup with a handheld blender or food processor. Add the grated cheese and stir well until it has melted and mixed into the soup.

Taste, and season with salt and freshly grated black pepper.

Butterbean, fresh herb & vegetable broth

This is a minestrone-type soup. It's comforting to begin with and then given character and a rich aroma by the generous helping of fresh herbs stirred in at the end.

Serves 6-8 depending on appetite

2 tbs olive oil

2 cloves garlic, crushed

200g red onions (one medium/large), peeled and diced ½ cm

200g leeks (one fattish one), halved lengthways and sliced ½ cm

200g carrots (2 medium/large ones), peeled, quartered lengthways and sliced ½ cm

2 sticks celery, halved lengthways and sliced ½ cm

2 tsp salt

2 x 400g tins butterbeans, including the liquid

1 x 500g packet passata

800ml water

1 dsp chopped fresh sage leaves

15g fresh dill, finely chopped

30g fresh parsley (curly or flatleaf) finely chopped

2 tbs soy sauce

Put the olive oil, garlic, red onion, leeks, carrots, celery and salt into a large pan and cook on a medium heat with the lid on for 20-30 minutes until all the vegetables are tender.

Add the butterbeans, passata and water. Bring to the boil and then simmer for about 10 minutes until everything is well amalgamated. Adjust the consistency with additional boiling water.

Stir in the finely chopped herbs and the soy sauce and season to taste with salt and black pepper.

Mushroom bisque

Here's a rich winter soup. The word 'bisque' indicates creaminess and spiciness. Add the earthy flavour of mushrooms and you have a winner. It may seem like a lot of mushrooms, but trust me (as Dr Who always says to his assistant before a disaster befalls).

I'm not normally a fan of dried dill or thyme, but they work well here.

Serves 6

500g onions (2 large), roughly chopped

2 tbs sunflower oil

2 tsp salt

1 tsp dried dill

½ tsp dried thyme

1 tsp paprika

½ tsp cayenne pepper

1kg mushrooms (whatever is good value), whole if small, chopped if big

½ litre water

½ litre milk

250ml sour cream

½ lemon, juice

dried thyme to garnish

Cook the onions with the oil and salt for about 10-15 minutes until they are soft.

Add the dill, thyme, paprika and cayenne pepper and stir well. Then add the mushrooms and cook on a medium heat until they are soft – this may take about 30 minutes depending on the size of your pan. If you have too many to fit in the pan all at once then add them in batches, letting each batch cook down as it is added.

Add the water and bring to the boil, then simmer for 5 minutes so that everything is well cooked and amalgamated.

Blend the soup to a purée with a stick blender. Add the milk, the lemon juice and ¾ of the sour cream, keeping a little back. Taste and season with salt and pepper and more lemon juice if necessary. Re-heat very gently to serving temperature, before garnishing each plate with the remaining sour cream and a sprinkle of dried thyme.

Curried spinach, potato & lentil soup

This is a sort of combination of two classic Indian curries in soup format – dahl and sag aloo. As it's not a blended soup, be sure to chop the potatoes and onions fairly small, so you can eat them with a spoon.

I'm not a fan of frozen vegetables in general but the two that we generally keep in our freezer at home are frozen peas and frozen spinach – probably indistinguishable from fresh spinach in this recipe, and more convenient. If you want the soup to be vegan, then add a bit more sunflower oil and miss out the butter. Using freshly toasted and ground mustard and cumin seeds adds extra zing – but use ready-ground if you're pressed for time.

The tamarind is a recent addition to this recipe. For me the sharpness adds another dimension – but if you're not familiar with tamarind maybe just use half the quantity at first, and then add more if it tickles your tastebuds.

Serves 6

3 tbs sunflower oil

50g butter

250g onions (one large), chopped 1cm

1 tsp salt

1 tsp mustard seeds, toasted and ground

1 tsp cumin seeds, toasted and ground

1 tsp turmeric

½ tsp ground cinnamon

¼ tsp cayenne pepper

¼ tsp ground ginger

150g red lentils

250g potatoes (one medium/large), diced 1cm (no need to peel)

1.5 litres water

2 tsp tamarind paste

350g frozen leaf spinach, de-frosted and chopped

In a large pan, cook the onion with the oil, butter and salt on a medium heat for about 10 minutes until the onion is soft, stirring occasionally to prevent sticking. Add all the spices except the tamarind paste and continue cooking for a couple of minutes, stirring constantly so it doesn't burn.

Add the lentils, diced potatoes and water. Bring to the boil and simmer with the lid on for 15-20 minutes, until the potatoes are soft but not quite falling apart (add more water if necessary).

Add the tamarind paste and spinach, bring back to the boil and simmer for another couple of minutes until the spinach is cooked and everything is well-amalgamated.

Check the consistency of the soup, adding more water if necessary. Finally, taste and season if necessary with salt and black pepper.

Sweet, spicy & chunky lentil & tomato soup

This is the kind of soup that is also a meal. As with other chunky soups it's worth taking the trouble to cut the vegetables in small neat pieces. You can substitute any other green speckled lentils for the puy lentils.

Serves 6

75g red lentils
75g puy lentils
150g potato (1 medium/small), diced
1.25 litre water

2 tbs olive oil
150g red onion (1 medium), diced finely
4 sticks celery, finely chopped
150g carrots (1 large), peeled and diced
2 tsp salt

1 red chilli, de-seeded and finely chopped
3 cloves garlic, crushed
4cm fresh ginger, peeled and finely chopped or grated

2 tsp turmeric
1 x 500g packet passata
2 tsp light muscovado sugar
1 tbs soy sauce
1 tsp white wine vinegar
1 x 250ml pack coconut cream
200g spring greens or cavolo nero, very finely shredded

Put both kinds of lentils and the potato in a pan with the water. Bring to the boil and then reduce the heat and simmer with the lid on for about 25 minutes until the puy lentils are tender (at which point the red lentils and the potato will also be soft).

Meanwhile, put the olive oil into another (large) saucepan, and then add the red onion, celery, carrots and salt and cook on a medium heat.

After 5 minutes add the chilli, garlic and ginger. Continue cooking for a further 10 minutes or so, stirring occasionally to prevent sticking and burning, until the vegetables are tender.

Add all the remaining ingredients, including the lentil/potato mixture (with cooking water), and bring back to the boil. Reduce the heat and simmer for about 5 minutes until the spring greens are tender.

Check the consistency of the soup and adjust with more water if necessary. Taste and season with salt, black pepper and more soy sauce or balsamic vinegar if you feel it needs it.

Chicken & sweetcorn soup

Pea & ham soup

Two soups made from leftovers

Chicken & sweetcorn, and Pea & ham

I would never make either of these recipes unless we have suitable leftovers from either roast chicken or smoked gammon, but they do make some of the best-tasting soups I know.

Serves 6 generously

Chicken & sweetcorn

1 litre chicken stock (see page 245)

400g large potatoes (if you've got leftover roast or boiled potatoes, use them), in 3 cm chunks, peeled or unpeeled

1 tsp salt

1 x 340g tin sweetcorn

200g leftover chicken meat, in ½ cm dice

1 lemon, zest and juice

Chicken & sweetcorn

Put the chicken stock and potatoes in a large pan with the salt and bring to the boil, then simmer until the potatoes are falling apart. Add half the sweetcorn. Whizz with a stick blender.

Add the rest of the sweetcorn, the diced chicken and the lemon juice and zest. Re-heat, check the seasoning and serve.

Pea & ham

175g split green peas

500ml ham stock (see page 225)

500ml apple juice

700ml water

150g leeks, halved, chopped and thoroughly washed

300g potatoes, in chunks

1 dsp chopped fresh mint leaves

200g smoked cooked gammon, finely diced

Pea & ham

Gammon stock is usually very salty so you're unlikely to need to add any salt in this recipe. Put everything apart from the mint and chopped ham in a large pan. Bring to the boil and simmer for an hour or more until the split green peas are very soft.

Add the mint leaves and cook for 5 minutes longer. Blend thoroughly. Add the chopped ham and re-heat.

Like a lot of soups made with pulses this soup tends to thicken up over time. Just add a bit of extra water when you're re-heating and then adjust the seasoning with salt (if needed) and possibly a squeeze of lemon juice.

Tart or quiche?

Quiche is a curious word. In smarter cafés than mine the same thing is renamed 'tart'. But when we tried calling it, for instance, a 'roast pepper and goats' cheese tart', then customers would point at it on the counter and say, 'do you mean the quiche?' So we've succumbed to the inevitable and 'quiche' it is.

The key to delicious quiche (and actually most food) is in the balance and the freshness. The freshness is simple but awkward. Simple because the only thing required is immediate consumption – but awkward because it's tempting for the home cook (or the lazy café cook) to think of making a quiche today that you want to eat tomorrow. But to my mind, re-heated quiche can never be quite as good as one fresh from the oven, and quiche eaten straight from the fridge seems pointless.

As far as balance is concerned, the main elements to balance are: pastry, eggs, cream, cheese plus the headline ingredient. And then some quiches will benefit massively from a boost of fresh herbs or mustard. For my cafés, the headline ingredient is usually a vegetable, often roasted or pre-cooked in some other way. There are also delicious quiches to be made with fish or meat, such as Quiche Lorraine (the original egg and bacon pie), or creations using chorizo or smoked salmon, but for these, you would need different proportions. But when vegetables are the star ingredients, as in the following recipes, the numbers are fairly universal.

With quiche fillings the world is your oyster. Most vegetables (apart, in my view, from brassicas which will end up smelling of over-cooked cabbage) can be used in quiches. Roast aubergines with tomatoes and basil; caramelized onions with thyme and Gruyère; roast red onions and potatoes with smoked cheddar; mushrooms with Stilton or Cashel Blue; courgettes with mint, sun-dried tomatoes and feta. The list could go on, but in this chapter I give four particularly delicious combinations, together with the recipe for the wholemeal pastry that I've used at the cafés for the last three decades.

Grumpy Old

Wholemeal quiche pastry

We use wholemeal pastry for our quiches. It's easy to work with, and the earthy nuttiness makes the perfect balance for rich creamy fillings. This pastry will come out wetter than you expect. But trust me – leave it in the fridge for a couple of hours and it will roll out beautifully and taste perfect.

Although I'm generally very pro-butter, we find that margarine (hard, block-type margarine) works equally well here. If you want to make this pastry vegan, use vegan margarine and no butter.

The quantities given here are for a 28cm-diameter loose-bottomed tart tin about 2.5cm deep. The balance of filling to pastry seems to work well and it makes a fairly large quiche (8 generous servings). But if you want to make a smaller one, try a 23cm-diameter tin (still 2.5cm deep) and use two-thirds of the ingredient quantities. You'll need to cut the cooking time by one-third too.

Makes 1 x 400g quantity of pastry

220g wholemeal flour

110g margarine or butter

60ml water

20ml sunflower oil

Pastry method

In a food processor whizz the flour and margarine/butter (or gently rub in using your fingers) until it resembles breadcrumbs. Add the water and sunflower oil and whizz/mix briefly until the pastry is just coming together. Tip onto your work surface and bring it together into a coherent blob. Cover with clingfilm. Chill for at least an hour before rolling out. If you're going to use it in the next couple of days put in the fridge – if not, store it in the freezer.

Making the quiche

To blind bake a tart shell: pre-heat the oven to 160°C (fan). Roll out the pastry and feed it into the corners of the tin (rather than stretching it). Press it tightly up the sides of the tin and then cut it off at the top. Over the pastry lay either heat-proof clingfilm or baking parchment and fill it with baking beans, either ceramic baking beans or simply dried beans such as the red kidney beans used here. Put in the oven for 20 minutes, then remove the beans and lining and continue to cook for a further 5-10 minutes until the pastry looks dry but has not started to go darker.

Make your filling (see pages 69-71) and pour it into the blind-baked pastry, spreading out the vegetables. Bake for 30-40 minutes at 150°C (fan) until the mixture is set and the top lightly browned.

Roast butternut squash,
ricotta & Parmesan quiche

Roast butternut squash, ricotta & Parmesan quiche

400g wholemeal pastry, baked blind – see page 67

800g butternut squash, peeled and diced 2cm

30ml olive oil

½ tsp salt

1 dsp fresh thyme leaves, stripped from the stalks

300ml double cream

4 eggs

250g ricotta

75g freshly grated Parmesan

Roast the diced squash in the olive oil and a little salt (30 minutes at 180°C fan) until the squash is colouring at the edges and quite soft.

Mix everything together except the Parmesan and pour into the blind-baked pastry. Sprinkle the Parmesan on top just before baking. Bake for 30-40 minutes at 150°C (fan) until the filling is set and the top looks nicely browned.

Leek, Gruyère & mustard quiche (probably my favourite)

400g wholemeal pastry, baked blind – see page 67

800g leeks, halved lengthways then sliced 2cm, thoroughly washed and drained

30ml olive oil

½ tsp salt

400ml double cream

5 eggs

225g grated Gruyère or Comté

2 tbs wholegrain mustard

Sweat the leeks in the olive oil with the salt in a covered pan on a low heat for about 10 minutes until just tender. Add all the other ingredients, pour into the blind-baked pastry, and bake for 30-40 minutes at 150°C (fan), until the top looks golden brown and the mixture is set.

Roast pepper, goats' cheese & fresh oregano quiche

Roast pepper, goats' cheese & fresh oregano quiche

400g wholemeal pastry, baked blind – see page 67

3 red peppers, in fat strips

2 yellow peppers, in fat strips

30ml olive oil

400ml double cream

5 eggs

225g fresh or mature goats' cheese

4 good sprigs fresh oregano, leaves stripped from the stalks

Roast the peppers in the olive oil and a little salt for about 25 minutes at 180°C (fan) until they are soft and beginning to colour.

Mix with all the other ingredients and pour into the blind-baked pastry. Bake for 30-40 minutes at 150°C (fan) until the filling is set and the top lightly browned.

Roast aubergine, tomato & basil quiche

400g wholemeal pastry, baked blind – see page 67

600g aubergine, diced 1cm

2 tbs olive oil (for the aubergine)

1 tsp salt (for the aubergine)

250g fresh plum tomatoes, 1cm dice

1 tbs olive oil (for the tomatoes)

½ tsp salt (for the tomatoes)

5 eggs

400ml double cream

225g grated cheddar or Parmesan or a mix of the two

15g fresh basil, leaves roughly torn

Heat the oven up to 180°C (fan). Making sure that you keep the aubergines separate from the tomatoes, toss them both with their olive oil and salt. Spread them out on separate baking trays and roast for 25-30 minutes until the aubergines are just going brown and are quite tender and the tomatoes are somewhat dried out.

Turn the oven back down to 150°C (fan).

Beat the eggs, then mix everything together and pour into the blind-baked pastry.

Bake for 30 to 40 minutes at 150°C (fan) until the mixture is set and the top is a rich brown.

Chicken & carbs

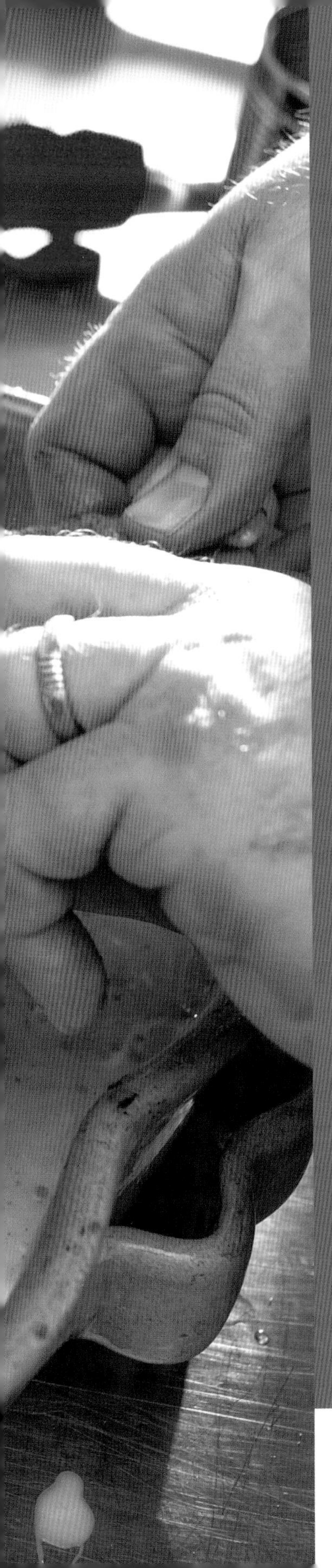

There is a miracle that happens when roast chicken juices mix with carbohydrates. I now almost always cook chicken on top of either rice or potatoes. Not a single bit of roast chicken juice is lost – it's all cooked into the accompanying carbs. This effect is magnified when the chicken is marinated and the chicken juices are enriched by spices or lemons. If you've not tried this method of roasting chicken pieces before, you're in for a treat. And whilst the chicken is good, the special bit is the accompanying rice or potatoes. At my cafés there's frequently a bidding war amongst the staff for any leftover bits of chickeny rice that haven't been served up with the chicken.

To get the best from this method we always use legs or thighs on the bone. Chicken breasts don't have enough fat on them and are too liable to dry out.

All the chicken and rice recipes will produce more rice than you'll really want with the amount of chicken. However, it's so delicious and re-heats so beautifully that it's worth making this amount and then you've got a ready-made delicious treat for the next day. Be sure to refrigerate any leftover cooked rice as soon as possible as cooked rice left for long periods at room temperature is a breeding ground for nasty bacteria. But if you don't like leftover delicious rice then reduce both the rice and liquid quantities by about one third.

Like a lot of the food we serve at the cafés, these are dishes for which most of the work is done well in advance – and that's also useful when you're cooking for friends at home so you're not fussing around in the kitchen when you want to be chatting with your pals.

Note that all the recipes in this chapter are best started the day before so that the chicken pieces marinate overnight.

Jerk chicken on rice & beans

Chilli roast chicken with lemon rice

Mexican chicken on lime rice with black beans

Tamarind & chilli chicken with coconut & lentil rice

Four variations on spicy chicken & rice

On the next page are four of my favourite variations on the spicy chicken and rice theme – but don't let this list restrict you… what about North African, Portuguese or Thai spicing? The world is your oyster.

With all the chicken and rice recipes in this chapter the rice goes in raw with the correct quantity of water or coconut milk and sometimes with extra beans or lentils. As the chicken cooks on top of it all the chicken juices cook into the rice. You end up with roast chicken with crisp, spicy skin on top of the most delicious chickeny aromatic rice. If you're not used to cooking rice from raw in the oven it can feel slightly unnerving the first time you do it. This is not only a good method for cooking chicken, it's probably the finest way of cooking rice.

Serves 6, or maybe only 3 teenagers

6 good-sized free-range chicken thighs or whole legs (1 piece around 275g per person is probably enough, though extra-hungry people may need 2 pieces each)

Buy free-range chicken thighs/legs

For the marinades

see individual recipes on the following spread

The night before

Mix all the marinade ingredients together, and put with the chicken in a big bowl. Work the marinade mixture into the chicken pieces thoroughly with your hands, cover with clingfilm and leave in the fridge overnight.

The next day

Put the chicken and all of the marinade into a deep baking dish such as you'd use for making lasagne (the same one that you'll end up serving it in) and cover with foil. The dish I use is 28cm x 28cm x 7cm deep. Roast at 160°C (fan) for about 30 minutes until the chicken is partly cooked. Note: this is only stage one: you'll cook the chicken again on top of the rice.

Take the chicken out and set aside.

Into the same dish, put the raw rice (and any extras such as lentils or beans), together with the measured quantity of liquid and salt.

Put the partly-roasted chicken pieces on top, skin side uppermost. Cook uncovered at 160°C (fan) for about 45 minutes until the rice is tender and the chicken skin is crisp and the chicken very well cooked.

Serve with a spicy or sweet relish such as roast pepper ketchup (page 241) and a simple salad. The carrot and green bean salad on page 131 is also delicious with these combinations.

Jerk chicken on rice & beans

One of the most delicious recipes I know. Try adding some roast pepper ketchup (recipe on page 241) and a simple salad and you've got a plate fit for a king.

See page 75 for the recipe method

The marinade

5g black peppercorns, freshly ground

¼ cinnamon stick, freshly ground

1 tsp fresh thyme leaves, freshly ground

2 bay leaves, freshly ground

2 tsp dried chilli flakes freshly ground (jalapeno are good)

1 tsp salt

1 tsp allspice

½ tsp mace

50g onion, finely chopped

3 tbs olive oil

½ lemon, juice of

To finish

400ml basmati rice

1 tsp salt

1 x 400g tin red kidney beans, drained

200ml tinned coconut milk or cream (either a 180ml can or half a 400ml can would be fine)

800ml water, boiling

Chilli roast chicken with lemon rice

This is good with cucumber raita (see page 246) and a simple salad, some green beans or cavolo nero tossed with butter and mustard (see page 131).

See page 75 for the recipe method

The marinade

2 chillies, de-seeded and finely chopped

40g root ginger, peeled and grated

4 cloves garlic, peeled and crushed

1 small onion, finely chopped

250g full-fat plain yoghurt

2 tsp garam masala

¼ tsp cayenne pepper

1 tsp cumin seeds, toasted and ground

1 tsp coriander seeds, toasted and ground

½ tsp hot smoked paprika

1 tsp turmeric

1 tsp salt

1 lemon, juice of

To finish

400ml basmati rice

2 lemons, juice of (this makes it quite lemony – use just one if you prefer)

800ml water, boiling

1 tsp salt

30g fresh coriander, roughly chopped, to serve

Mexican chicken on lime rice with black beans

This is a fairly hot recipe – just use one of the chipotle chillies if you like things a bit milder. If you can't find black beans then red kidney beans are fine.

We've had this at home accompanied by sour cream and a plain green salad with some fresh coriander in it. Some guacamole would also be good. And if you want to go all out spicy, the carrot and green salad (see page 131) would be perfect.

See page 75 for the recipe method

The marinade

5 cloves garlic, crushed

2 tsp salt

2 tsp cumin seeds, toasted and ground

2 dried chipotle chillies, soaked and finely chopped

½ tsp black peppercorns, ground

½ tsp dried oregano

2 tbs olive oil

To finish

400ml basmati rice

700ml water, boiling

1 x 400g tin black beans

100ml lime juice (juice of 3-5 limes depending on the size

1 tsp salt

Tamarind & chilli chicken with coconut & lentil rice

This is lovely but comes out fairly brown, so scatter the dish with plenty of chopped fresh coriander before serving.

See page 75 for the recipe method

The marinade

30ml sunflower oil

10g salt

50g tamarind paste

30g light muscovado sugar

2 chillies, de-seeded and finely chopped

3 cloves garlic, peeled and crushed

50g fresh ginger, peeled and finely chopped

To finish

100g puy lentils (or any speckled green lentils), cooked and drained

400ml basmati rice

800ml water, boiling

200ml coconut milk/cream

1 tsp salt

30g fresh coriander, roughly chopped, to serve

Mustard & garlic chicken on potatoes & onions

This recipe uses potatoes rather than rice to mop up the chicken juices. It's a really easy and stunningly delicious recipe to do for a big gathering. Thanks to Frances Leech for the original idea. Frances worked briefly in my cafés; she subsequently got a first at Oxford and a professional patisserie training in Paris, and now writes a delightful food blog at www.tangerinedrawings.com. We will undoubtedly hear more of Frances's food writing in the future.

Serve this dish with a simple green salad or some cabbage or green beans. This recipe is quite garlicky (as the title suggests) so feel free to reduce the garlic quantity if you don't like full-on garlic flavour.

Note that you should start marinating the chicken the day before you want to eat it.

Serves 6

6 good-sized free-range chicken thighs or whole legs (you're looking for around 275g per person)

The marinade

100ml crème fraîche

2 tsp salt

60g Dijon mustard

3 cloves garlic, crushed

The next day

1kg large potatoes, halved and very thinly sliced – no need to peel

500g large onions; quartered and thinly sliced

2 tbs olive oil

½ tsp salt

3 good sprigs thyme, the leaves pulled from the stalks

In a large bowl mix together the crème fraîche, salt, mustard and garlic and slather over the chicken using your hands to make sure that all the nooks and crannies of the chicken are fully coated. Cover with clingfilm and leave in the fridge overnight.

The next day, bring a large pan of water to the boil. When it's boiling add the sliced potatoes and bring back to the boil. Simmer for 3 minutes so the potatoes are partly but not completely cooked and drain.

Pre-heat the oven to 160°C (fan). Meanwhile in another pan sweat the onions in the olive oil and salt and the fresh thyme for about 15 minutes until they are very soft. Add the thinly sliced potatoes, stir thoroughly and take off the heat. Pour the onion and potato mixture into a baking dish, being sure to scrape in all the tasty fried onion. I use a round dish about 28cm diameter and about 7cm deep.

Arrange the chicken in its marinade on top of the veg, skin side up. The chicken pieces should be laid snugly against one another but not overlapping. Again, don't leave any marinade behind – scrape it all on top of the chicken.

Bake for 1-1½ hours. The skin should be crackly brown and the meat thoroughly cooked. Check that the potato is cooked. If necessary, turn the heat down and allow to continue cooking until the potato is really tender.

Celie's garlic & lemon chicken
with Charlotte potatoes

Celie is a proper cook who is used to cooking for large numbers. She's one of the first people I knew who kept a whole prosciutto ready for slicing when the need arose. I ate something similar to this chicken dish once at her house and have made it at home many times since.

Serves 6

1.5kg chicken thighs or legs, bone in and skin on – six very large thighs or six fairly modest legs

The marinade

2 lemons juiced, then skins chopped in 8 pieces, pips discarded

3 cloves garlic, finely chopped

a handful of sprigs of fresh thyme, leaves stripped from the stalks

75ml olive oil

2 tsp salt

The next day

500g large onions; quartered and thinly sliced

2 tbs olive oil

½ tsp salt

1kg Charlotte or other waxy salad potatoes e.g. Ratte or Pink Fir Apple, halved

4-12 hours before you want to cook the dish, mix the marinade ingredients together. Toss the chicken pieces very thoroughly in the marinade and leave covered in the fridge.

Half an hour before you want to cook the chicken, put the onion in a wide, deep, lidded pan. Cook in the olive oil and the ½ tsp of salt for about 25 minutes until the onion is very soft. Add the halved salad potatoes, stir well, put a lid on and cook for about 15 minutes, stirring regularly, so that the potatoes are nearly cooked.

Mix the onion and nearly cooked potato mix with the marinade, including the chopped lemon skins, and spread this out on the bottom of a large (28cm-diameter) roasting tray. Put the chicken pieces on top, skin side up. Cook for an hour at 160°C (fan) until the chicken skin is crisp, the flesh cooked and the potatoes completely tender. Serve straight from the roasting dish. If the skin isn't crisp enough turn the oven up to 200°C or more for a few minutes just to finish the crisping.

Lunch from the café ovens

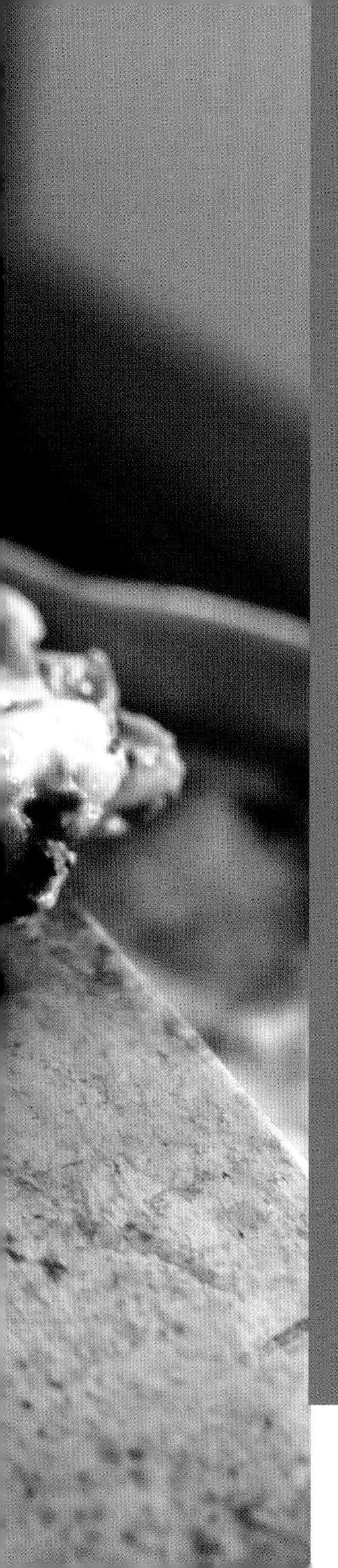

There is something about taking a bubbling lasagne or a golden crusted pie out of the oven and putting it on the table (or the counter in the cafés) that is both heart-warming and exciting. It's a moment of promise when you can smell the fizzling cheese or the beef and ale and your tastebuds begin to imagine the first mouthful. It's a little piece of theatre and perhaps my favourite moment of each café's day.

At 11.30am the quiches, pies, lasagne and gratins are just coming out of the ovens, the coriander is being sprinkled on the tagine and the rosemary roast potatoes are being transferred from their roasting trays to the warmed earthenware pot ready for service. It's a brief moment of expectant perfection before the hordes come and eat (thank goodness!).

One dish, the Courgette and feta filo pie, is historic; we served it on the day The Place Below opened in 1989 and I still love it. The combination of soft courgette, salty feta and crunchy pastry is as delicious now as it was then.

So this chapter is all about the food that emerges from the oven. Because it's all food that we serve from the café counters, these dishes can happily sit around in a warm place for a bit if you're not ready to eat at the precise moment they're cooked.

Within this chapter the gratins are all fairly quick to prepare, although they also need their 40 minutes or so in the oven. The other dishes (lasagne, pies, bakes and a moussaka) involve a bit more preparation-time and so the quantities given are for either 6 or 8 people.

Personally I would never go to all the trouble of making a beef and ale pie with its delicious cream cheese pastry or the lasagne each with 2 separate sauces, just to make enough for 2 or 4 people. I'd always make a slightly bigger quantity and either invite friends round to share it or have leftovers for another day.

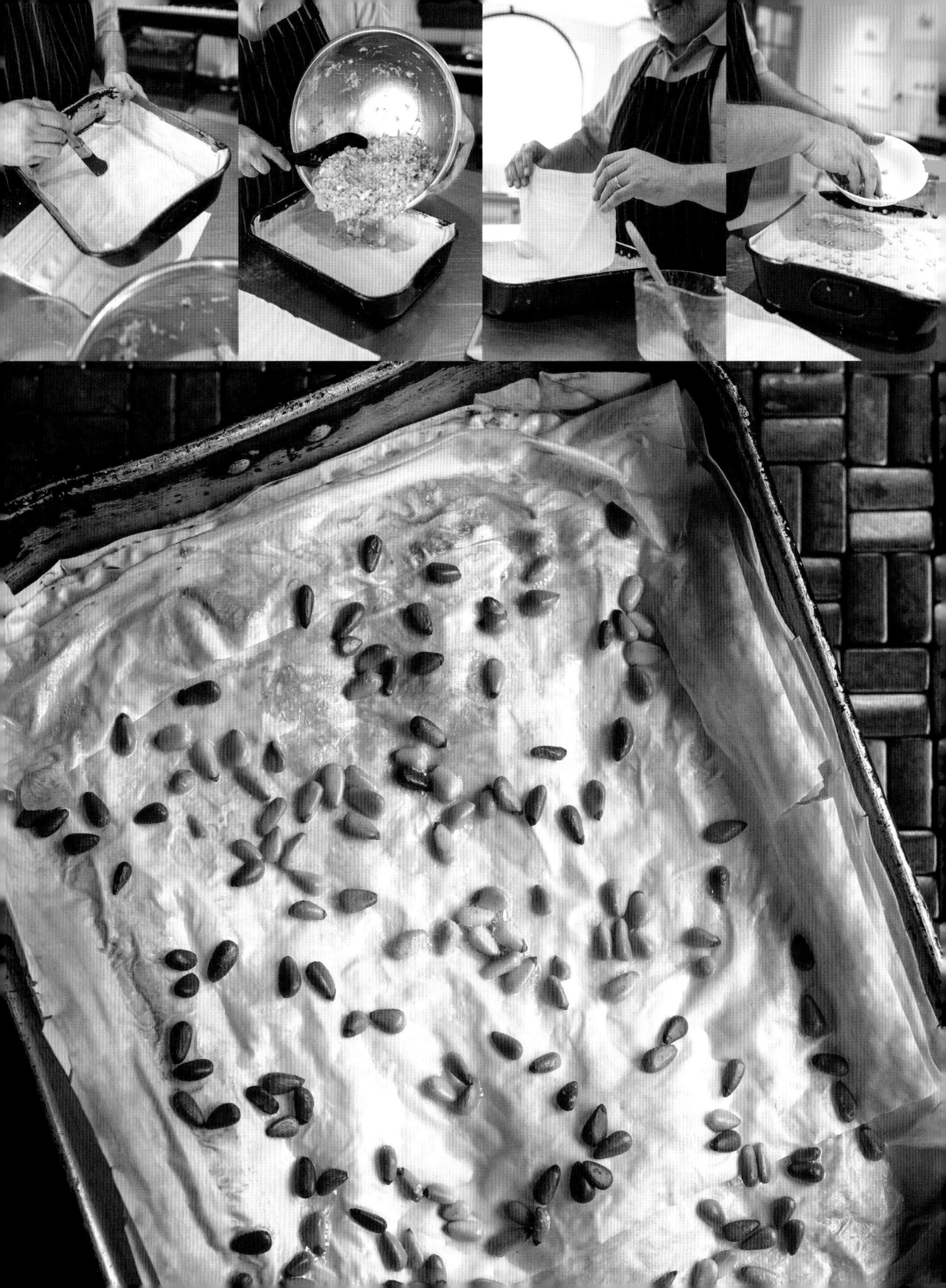

Courgette & feta filo pie

This is adapted from the excellent *Greens* cookery book from the celebrated vegetarian restaurant of the same name in California. We serve it regularly at the cafés with rosemary potatoes (page 238) and salad leaves and perhaps some roast pepper ketchup (page 241). But I particularly like it with patatas bravas (page 239).

Grating 1.5kg of courgettes is hard work if you don't have either a food processor with a grating attachment or alternatively a willing and able sous-chef.

When constructing the pie make sure that there is melted butter between each layer of filo pastry. This will ensure that your pastry is crunchy and delicious. Filo pastry is easy to work with when it is still damp and fresh from the pack, but has an irritating tendency to fall apart once it gets dry. So work quickly once you've got the pastry out of its wrapping, and if you get interrupted, cover the unused pastry with a damp cloth until you can return to it. Don't worry if the filo you're using isn't the same shape as the dish you're baking in. You can fold as necessary or have different sheets of filo starting on different edges. It doesn't matter if some bits of the pie have slightly more layers than others – just make sure there is melted butter between every layer.

Serves 6

For the filling

2 tbs olive oil

1.5kg courgettes, grated

1 tsp salt

150ml white wine

1 medium onion, diced ½ cm

4 eggs, lightly beaten

100g Parmesan, grated

200g feta, crumbled

For the pie

100g butter, melted

350g filo pastry

25g pine nuts (optional)

Heat the oil in a wide deep pan and then add the grated courgette and the salt. Cook, stirring regularly so that it all cooks evenly, until the courgette is soft. There will be a lot of liquid from the courgette, so drain well, retaining the courgette liquid.

Put the courgette liquid in a small pan with the white wine. Bring to the boil and boil fiercely with the lid off until the quantity has reduced by half. Mix back in with the courgette and with all the other filling ingredients.

Pre-heat the oven to 160°C (fan) and then assemble the pie. Brush the base and sides of a baking dish (28cm x 24cm or similar) with melted butter. Add the first sheet of filo pastry and then brush all over it with melted butter. Repeat for two more sheets. Then pour the filling into the dish and continue adding 4 further layers of pastry on top of the filling, with melted butter in between each sheet. Finish by sprinkling pine nuts on top of the pie.

Bake for about 35 minutes until the pastry is golden and the filling is just set.

Mushroom, Stilton & pumpkin pie

This is a rich but simple autumn pie. You can either use a good pumpkin such as Crown Prince, or butternut squash. This pie wants a very plain accompaniment such as green cabbage. If you're feeling particularly hungry add some boiled potatoes (Charlottes or Rattes) as well. I particularly like the rind of the cheese included in this as it melts to a delicious chewiness.

Serves 6

600g pumpkin or butternut squash, peeled and diced 2cm

1 tbs olive oil (for the pumpkin)

½ tsp salt

5 sticks celery, sliced 1cm

1 tbs olive oil (for the celery)

1 clove garlic, crushed

900g closed cap mushrooms – button or larger

1 tsp fresh thyme leaves, stripped from the stalks

200ml white wine

200ml double cream

150g Stilton, crumbled, including the rind

1 quantity cream cheese pastry – see page 251

egg wash (1 egg, lightly beaten with a pinch of salt for glazing)

Pre-heat the oven to 180°C (fan). Toss the diced pumpkin or squash in the olive oil and the salt, and roast on large baking sheets for about 30 minutes until very tender and just browning at the edges.

Put the celery, the second lot of olive oil and the garlic into a large saucepan and cook for 8-10 minutes until nearly tender. Add the mushrooms and the fresh thyme, cover the pan and, stirring occasionally, cook for another ten minutes with the lid on until they are soft. Drain well and keep the cooking liquid.

Put the mushroom liquid and the wine in a separate pan. Bring to the boil and boil fiercely until the volume is reduced by at least half. Add the double cream and bring back to the boil. Simmer until the sauce is a the consistency of fairly thick cream.

Add the sauce to the mushroom/celery mixture and the roast squash. Mix well and pour into a pie dish measuring about 28cm diameter. Sprinkle the crumbled Stilton on top.

Roll out the pastry, lay on top of the pie filling, and crimp the edges to the edge of the dish with your finger and thumb. Brush with egg wash.

Bake the pies at 160°C (fan) for about 40 minutes until the pastry is golden brown and the filling is piping hot.

Dean's beef & ale pie

Dean plans the menus at All Saints and his utterly delicious pie depends on a few seriously good ingredients. Buy properly aged shin of beef (or really good chuck steak if you can't get shin); shin takes a long time to cook but when the connective tissue has broken down it gives a gorgeous quality to the gravy. If you can get some bones to cook with the stew, this will add to the depth of flavour. Use dried ceps as well as field mushrooms; their earthy, musky aroma and soaking liquor goes beautifully with slow-cooked beef and the rich cream cheese pastry.

Serves 8

1kg shin of beef, diced

30g dried ceps

150g smoked streaky bacon
30g butter (for the bacon)
350g onion, roughly chopped
40g flour

250ml Stout, e.g. Guinness
150ml apple juice
1 tsp salt
1 dsp redcurrant jelly
2 bay leaves
2 sprigs thyme
(beef bones – optional)

600g flat mushrooms, in 3cm dice
35g butter (for the mushrooms)
one quantity cream cheese pastry – see page 251
egg wash (1 egg beaten with pinch of salt)

Brown the beef in batches in a large casserole dish. As each batch is browned set it on one side.

Meanwhile soak the ceps in enough hot water to cover them (you'll be using their soaking liquor later).

In the dish you browned the beef in, cook the bacon in the butter. When the fat is running, add the onion, cooking until it's soft.

Add the flour and cook on a low heat for 5 minutes, stirring regularly.

Add the beef, stout, apple juice, cep soaking liquor, salt, redcurrant jelly, bay leaves and thyme (plus beef bones if you have them), bring to the boil, put a tight-fitting lid on and simmer for 4 hours, either on a very low hob, or at 120°C (fan) in the oven. If it's a fan oven you need to check the liquid at least once an hour, and top up with boiling water if necessary.

Meanwhile, in a frying pan, fry the mushrooms in the second lot of butter on a high heat, until they are beginning to colour and give off their juice. Chop the rehydrated ceps and add them to the mushrooms.

When the meat has finished cooking, stir in the mushrooms with their cooking juices (discard the bones if you used them). Add seasoning as desired.

Put the stew into a large pie dish measuring 28cm x 28cm, or a round dish 28cm-diameter as illustrated here, and cover with the rolled out pastry, crimping firmly at the edges. Brush with egg wash and bake at 160°C (fan) for 40 minutes until the pastry is golden and cooked.

Venison & mushroom lasagne

Our Cambridge chef Lownz started making this dish when the Tudges (see supplier information on page 259) started offering him wild venison culled from the Mortimer Forest on the Herefordshire/Shropshire borders. It is really special when made with minced venison, but if you can't get hold of this, it's also an excellent recipe for a standard beef lasagne.

Serves 8

For the venison filling

1 medium onion, diced 1cm

1 clove garlic, crushed

2 tbs olive oil

1 tsp salt

600g minced venison (or beef)

4 sprigs of thyme, leaves left on the stalks

300g field mushrooms, diced 2cm

1 x 500g packet passata

25g dried ceps/porcini mushrooms

100ml hot water

For the cheese sauce

650ml milk

1 clove

1 bay leaf, broken

75g butter

75g white flour

75g grated cheddar

To assemble the lasagne

300g lasagne sheets

50g Parmesan, grated

75g soft breadcrumbs

Cover the ceps in hot water and leave to soak for 20 minutes or more. Cook the onions and garlic in the oil with the salt for about 10 minutes until the onion is soft. Add the minced venison/beef and the thyme and cook on a low heat with the lid on for about half an hour. Discard thyme stalks. Add the mushrooms, cook for about 5 minutes until softened a little, then add the passata. Take the ceps out of their soaking liquor, chop them finely, then add to the pan together with their soaking liquor. Simmer for a further 30-60 minutes until the sauce has thickened a little. Check the seasoning.

For the cheese sauce, heat the milk with clove and bay leaf until it begins to boil. Turn off the heat and leave for at least 10 minutes for it to take on the clove and bay leaf flavours. Remove the bay leaves and clove and bring the milk back to boiling point. Heat the butter in a large saucepan until it begins to foam, then tip in the flour and mix it well into the butter. When the mixture (the roux) begins to bubble and become paler in colour, begin adding the milk – to avoid lumps, add it a little at a time. After each addition of milk, bring the sauce back to the boil, then simmer and stir vigorously with a balloon whisk until thick and lump-free. When you have added all the milk, bring the sauce to the boil and immediately take off the heat. Stir in the grated cheddar and season to taste.

Pre-heat the oven to 160°C (fan). In a large deep baking dish (e.g. 28cm x 28cm x 5cm deep) add layers as follows: first a shallow layer of venison mix; lasagne sheets; cheese sauce. Then more lasagne sheets; venison; yet more lasagne sheets; and then cheese sauce. Finally mix the breadcrumbs and Parmesan and sprinkle over the top.

Bake for 40 minutes until the lasagne is tender and the top is beginning to brown. Allow to settle for 5 minutes before serving.

Roast vegetable & halloumi lasagne

Little nuggets of salty halloumi beautifully balance the rich béchamel and roast vegetables. You can vary the proportions of the different vegetables according to preference and availability.

Serves 8

For the roast vegetables

2 medium/large aubergines (about 600g), diced 1cm

100ml olive oil (for the aubergine)

1 tsp salt

2 red and 2 yellow peppers, diced 2cm

1 red onion, halved and thickly sliced

600g courgettes, sliced 2cm

For the tomato sauce

1 medium onion

2 tbs olive oil (for the onion)

1 tsp salt

2 cloves garlic, crushed

2 x 500g packets passata

30g fresh basil

For the white sauce

Use sauce recipe on page 91 but without the cheddar cheese

To assemble the lasagne

400g halloumi, diced 1cm

300g lasagne sheets

75g cheddar, grated

Pre-heat the oven to 180°C (fan). Mix the aubergine with the salt and olive oil. Spread on a large baking tray and roast for five minutes. Take out of the oven, toss with the peppers and onion and put back for 5 more minutes. Remove from the oven, mix in the courgette and then roast for 15 more minutes by which time the aubergine, peppers and onion should be browning and quite soft and the courgette should still be fairly firm. Set aside.

For the tomato sauce, fry the onion in the olive oil and salt. After about 5 minutes add the garlic. Stir well and continue cooking for another 5 or so minutes until the onion is soft. Add the passata and simmer for about 10 minutes. Take off the heat, add the basil and purée with a handheld blender. Mix with the roast vegetables.

Now you're ready to make the white sauce. Use the recipe from page 91 but leave out the cheddar cheese.

Pre-heat the oven to 160°C (fan). To assemble the lasagne, use a large deep baking dish (e.g. 35cm x 25cm x 4cm deep) and layer the lasagne as follows: start with a shallow layer of tomato/roast vegetables. Then add lasagne sheets; tomato/roast vegetables; halloumi; repeat with more lasagne sheets; tomato/roast vegetables; halloumi. Finish with a layer of lasagne; then the white sauce, and finally sprinkle grated cheddar on top.

Bake for 40 minutes until the lasagne is tender and the top is beginning to brown. Allow to settle for 5 minutes or so before serving.

Roast pepper, potato & goats' cheese gratin

This is a summery gratin. Because it uses salad potatoes (as opposed to the big floury ones that you'd mostly use for a gratin) it doesn't set in quite the same way. This is fine – enjoy the sloppy tomatoey creaminess. It's worth finding an interesting potato such as Ratte, Charlotte or Pink Fir Apple for this.

If you're going for more of a 'dinner party' presentation, divide the ingredients into 4 and make 4 little individual ovenproof dishes. You'll probably want to reduce the cooking time a little in this case.

It's a delightfully simple dish and just needs a green salad to go with it.

Serves 4

600g salad potatoes, halved lengthways

2 red and 1 yellow pepper, in fat strips

1 tbs olive oil

½ tsp salt

1 clove garlic, crushed

250g tomatoes (ideally plum tomatoes), diced 1cm

1 tsp fresh oregano leaves, roughly chopped (or substitute ¼ tsp dried)

350ml double cream

½ tsp salt

¼ tsp freshly ground black pepper

75g fresh breadcrumbs

75g grated cheddar

250g mature goats' cheese, e.g. Ragstone, diced 1cm

Bring a large pan of water to the boil and put in the halved potatoes. Bring back to the boil, simmer on a low heat for 10 minutes (the potatoes should be not quite cooked) and then drain.

Meanwhile pre-heat the oven to 180°C (fan). Toss the peppers in the olive oil and salt and roast for about 25 minutes until they are quite soft and beginning to brown at the edges. Mix the roast peppers with garlic, the sliced tomatoes, the chopped oregano and the almost cooked potatoes. Turn the oven down to 160°C (fan).

Warm the cream with the salt and pepper until nearly boiling. Mix the grated cheddar with the breadcrumbs.

Half fill a gratin dish measuring 20cm x 30cm with the potato/pepper mixture, then add a layer of half the diced goats' cheese. Then put another layer of the potato/pepper mix and another thin layer of goats' cheese. Pour the warmed, seasoned cream over and finish with the cheddar and breadcrumb mix.

Bake for about 40 minutes until it's bubbling and golden brown on top and the potatoes are really soft. If the top becomes too brown before the potatoes are cooked, cover the gratin with foil.

Time
and

Chicory, smoked ham & sweet potato gratin

This is currently my favourite gratin. It's a development of the classic bittersweet combination of chicory and ham. Whilst it looks pretty with the ham wrapped around large pieces of chicory and sweet potato, you actually get more delicious mouthfuls by dicing both the sweet potato and the ham. When we serve this in Cambridge we use Lincolnshire Poacher, a deliciously full-flavoured cheddar-type cheese, but of course good-quality cheddar is also fine.

Serve with either a chicory and orange salad (to continue the chicory theme) or some briefly boiled purple sprouting broccoli tossed in a bit of olive oil and lemon juice.

Serves 4

1kg sweet potato, diced 1cm

2 tbs olive oil

½ tsp salt

3 good -size chicory heads (about 450g), quartered lengthways

1 tbs olive oil

½ tsp salt

300ml double cream

½ tsp salt

¼ tsp freshly ground black pepper

150g thick-cut smoked ham, diced

100g strong cheddar, grated

Pre-heat the oven to 180°C (fan). Toss the sweet potatoes in a little olive oil and salt and spread on a baking sheet. Put in the oven and roast for 30-35 minutes until the flesh of the sweet potatoes is quite tender and beginning to brown in patches. Allow to cool completely.

Gently turn the chicory quarters in olive oil and salt and then roast for 10 minutes until they start to wilt.

Turn the oven down to 160°C (fan).

Heat the cream to not quite boiling, and add the salt and pepper.

Butter a gratin dish measuring 25cm x 35cm. Make a layer of half the sweet potato, half the ham and half the cream. Arrange the roast chicory on top of this and then put the rest of the sweet potato/ham/cream on top. Sprinkle the cheddar on top.

Put the dish in the oven and cook for 30-40 minutes until bubbling and irresistibly golden.

Bacon, cheddar & potato gratin

This is perhaps the ultimate comfort food, combining several of the world's finest ingredients: potatoes, cheese, bacon, garlic, wine and cream. A similar combination of ingredients produces various alpine dishes such as Tartiflette. Gruyère or Lincolnshire Poacher both make fine alternatives to cheddar.

This is pretty rich so just serve with salad leaves or a simple green vegetable – sweetheart cabbage (see page 235) or purple sprouting broccoli.

Serves 4

650kg potatoes, e.g. Maris Piper, halved and sliced 1cm but not peeled

350g smoked bacon, sliced into short thin strips

1 large onion, halved and sliced 1cm

1 clove garlic, crushed

150ml white wine

250ml double cream

150g cheddar or similar cheese, grated

Put the sliced potatoes in a large pan of boiling water, bring back to the boil and simmer for 5 minutes until partly cooked but not totally soft . Then drain (don't worry if you take it too far – your dish won't end up elegantly layered but it will still taste delicious).

Put the the bacon in a large frying pan and fry until very crisp. Remove the bacon and set aside but leave the fat in the pan.

Slowly cook the onion and garlic in the bacon fat. Keep cooking for about half an hour until the liquid is gone so it's almost a jam texture.

Add the wine and turn the heat up until the liquid has reduced to about 20% of its original volume. Then stir in the cream whilst still cooking. Bring to the boil and simmer for a couple of minutes until it thickens slightly.

Pre-heat the oven to 160°C (fan). In a gratin dish measuring 20cm x 30cm (or circular dish about 27cm diameter) put a layer of onion/cream on the bottom, then a layer of potatoes, then a layer of bacon.

Then add a bit more onion/cream, followed by a layer of cheese, then potatoes, then bacon.

Finally add the last of the onion/cream and put the rest of the cheese on top.

Bake for 30-40 minutes until golden and bubbling on top and the potatoes are completely tender.

Aubergine, potato & halloumi moussaka

Given a choice between a classic moussaka made with lamb mince and this version with halloumi, I'd often choose this version. It's rich and tasty and full of lively Greek flavours, and excellent on its own or with a simple green salad. I cook this in a fairly large lasagne-type dish measuring 28cm x 28cm and 7cm deep. But if you're cooking for fewer people, then reduce the quantities a bit and use a commensurately smaller baking dish.

Serves 6-8

For the vegetables and cheese

800g large potatoes, peeled and sliced ½ cm

800g aubergines, sliced about 1cm

100ml olive oil

salt and pepper

500g halloumi diced about 1cm

For the tomato sauce

30ml olive oil

400g onions, diced 1cm

2 good cloves garlic, crushed

1 tsp salt

2 x 400g packets passata

1 tbs chopped fresh oregano (or 1 tsp dried)

For the white sauce

650ml milk

100g butter

100g plain flour

500g Greek yoghurt

½ tsp salt

Put a large pan of salted water on to boil. Cook the potato slices in the water for about 10 minutes until soft but not falling apart. Drain and put to one side to cool.

Pre-heat the oven to 180°C (fan). Toss the aubergine slices with the olive oil and salt and freshly ground black pepper, then spread one layer deep in baking trays on baking parchment and roast until golden brown, about 15 minutes. Turn them over to brown on the other side for another 15 minutes. Put to one side.

In a large saucepan cook the onions and garlic in the olive oil and salt for about 15 minutes until the onion is soft. Add the passata and oregano. Bring to the boil, then simmer for about 20 minutes until the sauce has reduced by about a third.

Heat the milk in a pan until it is just coming to the boil, then remove from the heat. In another pan melt the butter and then stir in the flour. Cook over a low heat until the roux begins to bubble and becomes paler in colour. Then begin adding the milk. To avoid lumps, add the milk gradually. After each addition of milk bring the sauce back to the boil and stir until thickened and lump-free. When you have added all the milk, turn down the heat and stir in the yoghurt and the salt. Bring the sauce to the boil, stirring all the time, and then immediately take off the heat. Check the seasoning.

In your baking dish layer the aubergine slices, potato slices, halloumi chunks and tomato sauce. Try to fit in two layers of each. Finally, spread out the white sauce on top so that all the vegetables and tomato sauce are covered. Bake at 160°C (fan) for about 40 minutes until bubbling and golden brown on top. If it hasn't browned enough, turn the oven up to 180°C (fan) and leave for another 5-10 minutes to finish browning.

Lentil, leek & Parmesan bake

This is one of my favourite lunchtime recipes. The butter, lemon juice, leeks, Parmesan and white wine all take it a long way from an old-fashioned lentil loaf.

For the simplest meal serve it with some green leaves, or add some roast pepper ketchup (page 241). In late summer I love it with courgettes, tomatoes and basil (page 240) or spiced pepperonata (page 115).

Serves 6

350g red lentils

700ml water

1 tsp salt

125g butter

700g leeks, halved and then sliced 1cm, thoroughly washed and drained

100ml white wine

½ tsp cayenne pepper

50g butter

75g grated cheddar

150g grated Parmesan

2 eggs, lightly beaten

½ lemon, juice of

1 dsp fresh oregano leaves, roughly chopped (½ tsp dried oregano is ok if you can't get fresh)

500g tomatoes, sliced 1cm (one slice per portion)

60g Parmesan for the topping

Put the red lentils, the water and the salt in a large pan and bring to the boil. Then turn the heat down very low, put a lid on and simmer until the lentils are soft and there is no liquid (it's very easy to burn the bottom of the pan, so go carefully with this).

In a large pan with a lid, melt the butter; add the leeks and white wine. Bring to the boil, then turn the heat right down, put a lid on and simmer very gently for 8-10 minutes until the leeks are just tender. Take off the heat and drain over another pan, retaining the cooking liquid. Put the liquid in a small pan on a high heat without a lid and boil fiercely for 5-10 minutes until the volume of liquid has reduced by about half.

Mix the leeks, the reduced juices and all the other ingredients except the second lot of Parmesan and the sliced tomatoes. Pour the mixture into a baking dish measuring about 28cm x 28cm. Arrange the sliced tomatoes on top and sprinkle with the last of the Parmesan.

Bake at 160°C (fan) for about 45 minutes until set and beginning to brown.

5 wholesome hotpots (& they all happen to be vegan)

When I first worked in a tiny vegetarian café in the early 80s, each day we made a vast pot of one of four sauces (tomato, brown, white or a rather dodgy sweet-and-sour) and then boiled a selection of vegetables to stir into them. This provided filling and vaguely tasty gloop for the local office workers in Westminster but precise and careful food it was not.

Our hopes and expectations of plant-based cookery have come a long way since then. Making delicious vegan casseroles requires similar skills to making great soups. You want to create a balance of sweet, sour, salty, spicy and creamy. You need good base notes of tomato, soy and wine balanced with top notes from fresh herbs and other aromatics added right at the end. And you're looking for varying textures – chickpeas, roast aubergines and cauliflower or roast pumpkin and sugar snap peas.

Personally I don't feel that I've had a proper meal unless there's some protein in it, so all of these dishes provide a bit of that as well as really full-on delicious flavours.

All the dishes are fairly simple – but it makes all the difference to take care with each step. The peppers and aubergines must both be sufficiently roasted and seasoned; the onion must be cooked for long enough; don't skimp on the garlic or ginger; don't overcook the cauliflower (or make the florets too large); be sure to taste and adjust the seasoning at the end. There's nothing complicated – but every step matters.

Most of these dishes make perfect starting points for exploration and experimentation, and easily become dishes for feasting! My niece Grace got married from our house last year and for her pre-wedding lunch she and her friends made a version of the aubergine and lentils and the Thai pepperonata with some Cashel Blue stirred in, served with Alex Gooch's focaccia. It all went down very well and kicked off a wonderful weekend of celebrating which, entertainingly, somehow found its way into the magnificently titled 'Perfect Wedding' magazine!

Roast aubergines & lentils

in a balsamic coconut sauce

This is a vegan version of a recipe which appears in my first book, *Food From the Place Below*. Double cream is here replaced with coconut cream, and the roast sweet potatoes are a new addition. It goes beautifully with the spiced pepperonata (page 115) and either plain rice or some creamy mash.

The portion sizes given here allow for the casserole to be served with rice or other grain alone. If you are serving this with the spiced pepperonata then you may want to reduce the quantities below slightly.

Serves 6

600g sweet potato, diced 1cm
25ml olive oil (for sweet potato)
½ tsp salt
1kg aubergines, diced 1cm
75ml olive oil (for aubergines)
another 1 tsp salt

300g puy lentils (or any speckled green lentils)

30ml olive oil (for onions)
500g onions, halved and sliced ½cm
½ tsp salt
1 chilli, de-seeded and finely chopped
3 cloves garlic, crushed

30ml balsamic vinegar
45ml soy sauce
1 x 400ml tin coconut milk
30g flat parsley, roughly chopped
30g fresh basil, roughly chopped

Pre-heat the oven to 180°C (fan). Toss the sweet potato in the olive oil and salt. Spread onto a baking sheet and roast for about 35 minutes until very soft and beginning to brown. Toss the aubergine in olive oil and salt. Spread onto a couple of baking sheets and roast for about 30 minutes until the aubergine is browned and very tender.

Boil the lentils for about 30 minutes in plenty of water until they are just tender but not collapsed, then drain.

Meanwhile in a large Le Creuset-type heavy-bottomed pan (the one that you'll end up serving the dish from), cook the onion in olive oil and salt. After about 5 minutes add the chilli and garlic and continue cooking on a medium heat for about 15 minutes more until the onion is really soft.

To the onion mix add the roast aubergine and sweet potato, the cooked and drained lentils and the balsamic vinegar, soy sauce and coconut milk. Bring just to the boil and simmer on a very low heat for about 5 minutes until the flavours have mixed nicely. Stir in the parsley and basil. Check the seasoning and serve.

Roast aubergine ratatouille

Some of my cooking is firmly rooted in the late 1980s and early 1990s, and this dish is the classic example. Roasting peppers and aubergines was a constant feature then and has become a staple in my cooking. In those days using generous quantities of basil, flat leaf parsley (or continental parsley as it used to be called) and olive oil felt like a new world order. Now it just seems normal and delicious.

We have sold huge quantities of what we continue to describe on our menu as 'roast aubergine ratatouille', served with everything from plain rice to pesto mash or tabouleh and garnished with spiced chickpeas (page 243), chilli roast tofu or buffalo mozzarella. Nowadays I also find it a great accompaniment to roast lamb or roast belly pork.

Serves 6 as a main dish

For the vegetables

750g aubergine, diced 1.5cm

4 tbs olive oil (for the aubergine)

1 tsp salt

2 red peppers, in fat strips

2 yellow peppers, in fat strips

1 tbs olive oil (for the peppers)

pinch salt

600g courgettes, cut in diagonal slices about 1cm thick

1 tbs olive oil (for the courgette)

pinch salt

For the sauce

1 very large or 2-3 medium onions (about 400g total), halved and sliced

50ml olive oil

½ tsp salt

2 cloves garlic, crushed

2 x 500g packets passata

30g basil

30g flat leaf parsley

Toss the vegetables (separately) in olive oil and salt, then spread out onto baking sheets. Roast at 180°C (fan) as follows, keeping them separate as they take different lengths of time: aubergine for 30 minutes, until colouring at the edges and very soft; peppers for 25 minutes, until beginning to brown at the edges; courgette for 20 minutes, until just beginning to brown but still fairly firm.

For the sauce, in a large pan (a Le Creuset-type heavy-bottomed casserole dish is perfect) fry the onion gently in the olive oil with the salt on a medium heat. After about 5 minutes add the crushed garlic and continue cooking for a further 15-20 minutes. Make sure the onion is very soft and cooked down, then add the passata and bring to the boil. Continue simmering gently with the lid off for about half an hour until the sauce is reduced by about one third – you want to create a thick sauce rather than a wet and sloppy one. Take off the heat.

Chop the basil and parsley and stir into the sauce together with all the roast vegetables – do this right at the end, as soon as you've finished cooking, for maximum aroma.

Check the seasoning and serve. If possible serve ratatouille warm rather than piping hot – the flavours work much better like that.

Aubergine, chickpeas & cauliflower
in a chilli & preserved lemon tomato sauce

Nearly all spicy dishes have a long list of ingredients and this dish is no exception but it's still simple to make. The preserved lemon and barely cooked cauliflower give it its particular character. Serve with plain basmati rice.

Serves 6

600g aubergine, diced in 2cm pieces

50ml olive oil (for roastiing)

salt and pepper

3 peppers (red and yellow), in fat strips

2 cloves garlic, peeled and roughly chopped

1 walnut-sized piece of fresh ginger, peeled and roughly chopped

1 tsp coriander seeds, toasted and ground

1 tsp cumin seeds, toasted and ground

1 tsp turmeric, ground

2 red chillies, de-seeded and finely chopped

25ml olive oil (for the chilli paste)

1 small cauliflower in small florets with the stalk finely sliced

1 large onion, peeled, halved and sliced

25ml olive oil (for the onion)

500g passata (or puréed tinned tomatoes)

½ a preserved lemon, finely chopped

450g tin chickpeas

small bunch fresh coriander (about 30g), roughly chopped

Begin by roasting the diced aubergines. Toss them with about half of the 'roasting' olive oil and the salt and pepper and roast on baking sheets at 180°C (fan) for about 30 minutes until soft and well-browned around the edges. Put to one side. Repeat this process with the peppers, which will only take 25 minutes.

Make the chilli paste by blending together the garlic, fresh ginger, toasted and ground coriander and cumin seeds, turmeric, chopped chillies and 25ml olive oil.

Cook the cauliflower florets in plenty of boiling water until just tender. This will only take about a minute if you are using a big pan of water with not too much cauliflower. Drain the florets and put straight into cold water. As soon as they are cold drain again and put aside.

Cook the onion in a very large pan (relative to the amount of onion you are cooking) in the last 25ml of olive oil over a low-ish heat, until the onion is soft but not browned.

Add the passata, the chilli paste and the preserved lemons. Drain the chickpeas but keep the liquid and add half of it to the pan. Simmer over a medium heat until the sauce has reduced by about a third.

Add the roast aubergines and peppers, chickpeas and cauliflower, stirring everything together. Heat through thoroughly. Taste and add salt and black pepper as necessary. If you'd like the dish a bit wetter, then add the rest of the chickpea water. Use the chopped coriander to garnish each portion as you serve it.

Thai red curry with pumpkin

This is a sweet and fairly mild curry which started life with a Thai/Mexican chef who worked at The Place Below over 20 years ago; it has been gently evolving ever since. It's best served with plain basmati rice, nothing more.

Serves 6

For the red curry paste

4cm knob of fresh ginger, grated

2 sticks lemongrass, finely chopped

4 cloves garlic, crushed

1 tsp dried chilli flakes

1 tsp salt

1 tbs sunflower oil

2 red peppers, de-seeded and chopped

30g fresh coriander, roughly chopped

30g Thai basil (or ordinary basil), chopped

For the curry

1 medium butternut squash or pumpkin, approx. 1kg, peeled and diced 2cm

2 tbs sunflower oil (for the squash)

1 tsp salt

1 medium red onion, peeled, sliced ½ cm

600g carrots, sliced thinly and diagonally

1 tbs sunflower oil (for the onion)

1 x 400g tin coconut milk

1 tbs palm sugar or light muscovado sugar

200g sugar snap peas

1 lime, juice and zest

1 small red onion, finely sliced, to garnish

30g fresh coriander, roughly chopped

50g red-skinned peanuts, toasted

Put the ginger, lemongrass, garlic, chilli flakes and salt in a pan with the sunflower oil and cook on a low heat for about 10 minutes until very soft. Add the peppers and continue to cook for another 10 minutes, still on a low heat, with the lid on until the peppers are also very soft. Take off the heat and add the roughly chopped coriander and basil. Whizz to a purée with a handheld blender. Set on one side.

Toss the pumpkin/squash cubes with the sunflower oil and salt. Roast on baking sheets for 30-35 minutes at 180°C (fan) until tender and slightly browned around the edges. Put to one side and leave to cool.

While the pumpkin/squash is roasting, put the red onion, carrots and sunflower oil in a casserole dish and cook over a low-ish heat until just tender. Add the coconut milk, sugar, roast pumpkin and raw sugarsnap peas and lime juice and zest. Stir very gently so that the squash/pumpkin doesn't fall apart too much. Turn up the heat and bring the curry nearly to the boil (the coconut milk may curdle if it boils). Stir in the red curry paste and continue to cook over a very low heat for about 5 minutes until the sugar snaps are barely cooked and the curry is slightly thickened. Check the seasoning and adjust as necessary with salt and lime juice.

For the garnish, mix together the uncooked red onion, the chopped coriander and the toasted peanuts and garnish each helping with a generous spoonful.

Thai-spiced pepperonata

This is a really sharply flavoured dish that I think works particularly well as an accompaniment to the aubergine and puy lentil casserole on page 107. Its intense flavour means that you don't want a huge amount per person – it's halfway between a relish and a side dish.

Serves 6 as an accompaniment

2 red peppers, in fat strips

2 yellow peppers, in fat strips

25ml olive oil (for the peppers)

½ tsp salt

250g onion, halved and sliced fairly thinly

25ml olive oil (for the onion)

½ tsp salt

1 stick lemongrass, finely chopped

1 chilli, de-seeded and finely chopped

2 cloves garlic, crushed

4 cm knob ginger, peeled and grated

1 x 500g packet passata

1 lime (all the zest and half the juice)

30g fresh coriander, roughly chopped

30g Thai basil (or ordinary basil) roughly chopped

Pre-heat the oven to 180°C (fan). Toss the peppers in the olive oil and the salt. Spread onto a couple of baking sheets and roast for about 25 minutes until the peppers are browning at the edges and going soft.

In a medium saucepan cook the onions in the olive oil and salt on a medium heat. After about 5 minutes add the lemongrass, chilli, garlic and ginger and continue cooking for about 15 minutes more until the onion is really soft. Add the passata to the onions, stir together and then bring to the boil. Turn down the heat and simmer until reduced by about a quarter.

Stir in the roast peppers and keep cooking gently for a couple of minutes until the peppers are thoroughly hot again. Finally stir in the lime juice and zest and the chopped basil and coriander. Taste and add salt and black pepper as necessary and serve.

Salads & things to go with them

Salads of all shapes and sizes are wonderful as long as they are made with love and generosity. I hate the idea of salad as something you 'should' be eating, to go along with the hunk of meat that you really want to eat. Salads for me are multi-sensual pleasures. The sight, the taste, the textures, the aromas should all be a delight. Green leaves glistening with a classic vinaigrette; roast cubes of aubergines nestling up to plump raisins and parsley; roast peppers and courgettes with a basil-laden tomato dressing.

For me salads fall into two categories: salad-bowl-type salads which are served as part of a salad plate or as an accompaniment to other main dishes; and what the French call 'salades composées', presented on individual plates in a more 'cheffy' manner, often with some protein such as smoked duck breast, bresaola or Parmesan shavings on top.

This chapter is basically about 'bowl salads', which is what we serve at the cafés and what tends to work well for big parties at home. Not only are they good for large numbers of people, but the recipes here are all fairly robust and can be kept overnight in the fridge, to serve happily the next day. If you're doing this, don't forget to take them out of the fridge an hour or two before you want to eat them as all salads are nicer at room temperature than fridge-cold.

At home we eat quite a lot of the other kind of salad, the 'salade composée' or 'plated salad'. This is what my son Jonathan used to call a 'not salad' because it tends to have lots of things he approved of (roast chicken, Parmesan shavings, roast peppers) and not much of the green leafy stuff.

In addition to the salad bowls I've also included delicious hummus and baba ganoush recipes, because you want to have at least one of them on the table for any big summer salad feast.

Hummus
Baba ganoush

Baba ganoush (charred aubergine purée) & Hummus

Baba ganoush and hummus have become staples of life. But they're frequently not as good as they should be, so I feel these excellent recipes are worth repeating. They're both delicious as dips with spianata or as part of a summer salad or sandwich, or on a meze platter. And the baba ganoush is sensational with slow-cooked pulled lamb (page 163) and ripe tomatoes.

For the baba ganoush

800g aubergine (about 2 medium-sized aubergines)

1 small clove garlic, crushed

150g pale tahini

2 lemons, juice of

150ml olive oil

1 tsp salt

For the baba ganoush

Cook the aubergines over an open flame. This is most easily done on a gas hob but can also be done under the grill. The point is to char the skin completely. To achieve this properly will probably take 10-15 minutes on a fierce gas flame, turning the aubergine as soon as each side is scorched and collapsed. Don't worry about going too far; it is virtually impossible to overdo the burning process. See the picture on page 116.

Leave the charred aubergines to cool. When they are cool, gently remove the skin. You will find that little flecks of burnt skin remain. This is fine and will add to the flavour, but you want to get rid of all substantial bits of skin and the stalk.

Purée the peeled flesh with all the other ingredients in a food processor. Taste to check the seasoning and adjust as necessary.

For the hummus

400g can of chickpeas, drained (keep the liquid)

30g pale tahini (a generous tablespoon)

1 tsp salt

1 lemon, juice of

½ garlic clove, crushed

70ml extra virgin olive oil

For the hummus

To make the hummus, place all the ingredients except the olive oil in a food processor. Add 80ml of the reserved liquid from the chickpeas and process until smooth. With the motor still running, pour in the olive oil. If it is too thick add a little more of the reserved cooking liquor. I like it on the creamy and liquid side – the texture of very thick cream. Taste to check the seasoning and adjust as necessary.

Tabouleh

Tabouleh is a dish much more often made badly than well. Typically it consists of some under-seasoned couscous with a tiny smattering of herbs, served too cold straight from the fridge. If that's what you've experienced before then think again. Tabouleh should be bursting with parsley, mint, lemon juice, garlic and olive oil and should always be served at room temperature – unless you want it slightly warmer to accompany a tagine or ratatouille.

The proportions given here are still probably slightly timid regarding the herbs – in Lebanon it's more like a parsley and mint salad with a little grain added – but for me the balance is right and gives it enough of a carbohydrate base to work well both as part of a meze or as an accompaniment to spicy stews. For a rougher texture, coarse-grained bulghur wheat is an excellent alternative to couscous.

Serves 6 as an accompaniment or as part of meze

375ml boiling water

250g couscous

1 tsp salt

1 small clove garlic, crushed

30g fresh mint, stripped from the stalks

30g flat leaf parsley (curly parsley is perfectly fine as a subsititute)

125ml olive oil

2 lemons, juice of

Put the couscous and salt into a large bowl, and pour the boiling water over it (I'd have the bowl sitting on a set of scales and measure as I pour from the kettle). Cover the bowl and leave for 5-10 minutes, then fluff up with a fork.

Chop the mint and parsley – I like them chopped medium-fine for this. You're certainly not looking for the sort of parsley dust that fancy cookery schools get you to create for garnishing dishes.

Mix everything together. If you're not eating the tabouleh immediately and you're storing it in the fridge, be sure to bring it out in plenty of time to come back to room temperature before serving.

Bulghur & chickpeas in a soy vinaigrette

This is a variation on 'Bart's salad' from my old friends Ian and Nick's former restaurant in Ashtead in Surrey. It may not look thrilling, but tastes delicious, and it will open your mind to the many possibilities of bulghur wheat. Serve as part of a salad selection or try it warm as a side dish with ratatouille.

Serves 6-8 as an accompaniment or part of a mixed salad plate

250g coarse bulghur wheat
650ml boiling water

100g raisins
1 x 400g tin chickpeas, drained
60g flat leaf parsley, roughly chopped
2 tbs Dijon mustard
2 tbs white wine vinegar
4 tbs soy sauce
150ml olive oil

Put the bulghur wheat and the measured amount of boiling water in a lidded pan. Bring to the boil and simmer on a very low heat with the lid on for 5-8 minutes until all the water has been absorbed (if you are using fine bulghur wheat or couscous, which are both good alternatives, then just soak in the boiling water rather than simmering).

Allow the bulghur wheat to cool and then mix well with all the other ingredients.

Roast pepper & courgette salad
with tomato dressing & feta

If carrot salads and coleslaws are made for winter then roast pepper and courgette salads are perfect for summer and early autumn.

You can use thinly shaved or spirallized raw courgettes instead of roast chunky ones if you want – a good alternative for when you've got sparklingly fresh courgettes. And you don't have to follow this recipe to the letter – a mixture of red and yellow cherry tomatoes, for instance, in place of diced large tomatoes, would be both pretty and tasty.

Serve this with either tabouleh (see page 121) or some spianata (see page 31) and you've got a perfect summer lunch.

Serves 6 as a main dish

3 peppers (red and yellow mixed) in fat strips

2 tbs olive oil (for the peppers)

½ tsp salt

500g courgettes, in chunks

2 tbs olive oil (for the courgettes)

½ tsp salt

35g sun-dried tomatoes in oil, chopped very fine

30g basil

1 tbs balsamic vinegar

3 tbs olive oil (for the tomatoes)

500g fresh tomatoes, diced

250g feta, crumbled

Pre-heat the oven to 180°C (fan). Mix the peppers with 2 tbs of olive oil and ½ tsp of salt and spread on a baking sheet and roast for 25 minutes until tender and colouring at the edges. The skin should be beginning to wrinkle.

Mix the courgettes with 2 tbs of olive oil and the other ½ tsp of salt and spread on a baking sheet and roast for 20 minutes until just beginning to colour but still fairly firm.

In a small blender whizz together the sun-dried tomatoes, basil, balsamic vinegar and 3 tbs olive oil.

Allow the veg to cool and then mix in the diced fresh tomatoes and everything else except the crumbled feta. Gently stir in the feta just before serving.

Fattoush with fresh goats' cheese

This Lebanese salad is full of zesty summer herbiness. Like many middle-eastern salads, generous use of herbs is essential. The goats' cheese is not traditional but makes a meal of what otherwise feels like a side dish to me. The Perroche cheese from Neal's Yard Creamery is the perfect ingredient here, but if you can't get hold of fresh goats' cheese, feta also works well. You could try using spianata (page 31) in place of pitta, it's delicious!

It's worth peeling and de-seeding cucumbers for this recipe as it keeps the salad from becoming too wet.

This is a perky and delicious salad but it is completely spoiled if you overcook the cauliflower – so put a timer on when you put the cauliflower in the boiling water.

Serves 6

300g pitta or flatbread

2 tbs olive oil (for the pitta/flatbread)

300gm cauliflower, in tiny florets, stems very finely sliced

1 cucumber, peeled, quartered lengthways, de-seeded and sliced

250g cherry tomatoes, halved

50g spring onions, finely sliced

3 sticks celery, finely chopped

100g radishes, quartered

30g fresh mint leaves, roughly chopped

30g fresh coriander, roughly chopped

60g flat leaf parsley, roughly chopped

1 clove garlic, crushed

2 lemons, juice of

2 tsp sumac

150ml olive oil

250g fresh goats' cheese

Pre-heat the oven to 180°C (fan). Toss the pitta or bread in the first lot of olive oil, place on a baking sheet and bake for about 15 minutes until crisp. Break into bite-sized pieces.

Meanwhile, bring a large pan of water to the boil. When it's boiling add the cauliflower and cook for 1 minute (no longer) – then drain.

Mix everything together except the fresh goats' cheese. Divide onto plates and then garnish each plate with the crumbled cheese.

Roast aubergine, pine nuts & raisins
with balsamic dressing

This is a rich and delicious salad that works well as a starter on bruschetta and equally as part of a salad plate, perhaps with tabouleh (page 121) or the bulghur wheat salad (page 123) and the roast pepper salad (page 125).

Be sure not to undercook the aubergines. Aubergines are always unpleasant and rubbery when undercooked but this is particularly so in a salad.

This salad is particularly good served when the aubergine is still slightly warm. If you've stored it in the fridge be sure to allow it to come to room temperature before serving.

It may sound like a lot of olive oil but as long as the aubergine is tossed properly with the oil and salt before roasting, the oil will be absorbed and become part of the deliciousness of this dish.

Serves 6 as a starter or part of a mixed salad plate

1 kg aubergine (about 3 medium ones), diced 1cm

175ml olive oil (for the aubergine)

1 tsp salt

2 tbs balsamic vinegar (nothing fancy necessary)

50g pine nuts, toasted until golden

50g raisins

60g flat leaf parsley, roughly chopped

2 tbs olive oil

Pre-heat the oven to 180°C (fan). In a large mixing bowl toss the diced aubergine with the olive oil and salt and spread out onto baking trays. Use as many trays as necessary so that the aubergine is only one layer deep. Roast the aubergine for about 30 minutes until it is browning at the edges and completely soft. Allow it to cool for at least 5 minutes.

Toss everything together.

Carrot salad with cauliflower & sun-dried tomato dressing

Cauliflower has become a fashionable vegetable. Prepare it in small florets or sub-florets and use the tender part of the stalk, but slice it very finely. Cook the cauliflower very briefly, and don't let it sit around keeping warm.

Serves 6-8

40g sun-dried tomatoes in oil

1 clove garlic, peeled and crushed

1 chilli, de-seeded and roughly chopped

1 lemon, juice of

40ml olive oil (or oil from the dried tomatoes)

1 small or ½ a medium cauliflower broken into florets, with the tender part of the stalk very finely sliced. You want about 300g of prepped cauliflower

500g carrots, finely grated

25g red onion, very finely diced (optional)

50g raisins

1 small bunch (approx. 50g) flat parsley, roughly chopped

Put the first five ingredients in a blender and whizz.

Bring a large pan of water to the boil. Add the prepared cauliflower florets and finely sliced stalk. Cook for 1 minute and then drain and toss with the dressing. Allow to cool.

Add the grated carrot, red onion, raisins and parsley and mix everything very well together.

Spicy carrot salad with green beans & Ottolenghi dressing

The chilli paste in this recipe will keep in the fridge for several weeks and works as an all-purpose generator of spicy flavour. Alternatively, you could use ready-made harissa paste, but this can be a bit insipid. This tasty dressing is adapted from a Yotam Ottolenghi salad.

Instead of fine beans you could substitute runner beans or other local green beans. Runner beans should be sliced very finely and boiled only very briefly. Blanched green cabbage instead of beans is also good.

Serves 6 generously

200g fine green beans, topped, tailed and halved

4 tbs sunflower oil

300g onion (1 large one), halved and sliced

1 tsp chilli paste (see page 247 for recipe)

½ tsp salt

½ tsp sugar

50ml white wine vinegar

600g carrots, peeled and finely grated

Boil the green beans until they are just tender (3 minutes or so) and then drain.

Meanwhile heat half the oil in a pan and cook the onions until golden brown.

In a salad bowl, whisk the chilli paste with the salt, sugar, vinegar and the remainder of the sunflower oil, making sure that the spice paste is completely broken up and amalgamated. Add the onion, grated carrot and green beans and mix everything together.

Carrot salad with celeriac & lemon, honey & dill dressing

This is a sweet and fragrant salad, light years away from the potentially cloying classic celeriac remoulade. There's quite a lot of grating to do, so it's probably worth getting out the electric grater if you've got one.

The only skill involved in this recipe is mixing – in my view an underrated art. This is particularly important if you're making a bigger quantity of a salad such as this. It's very disappointing to get a bit of dried up grated carrot when it should all be beautifully dressed.

This will keep very happily in the fridge for a couple of days.

Serves 6 generously as an accompaniment or as part of a mixed salad plate

500g carrots, peeled and grated

1 small celeriac (about 600-800g) peeled and grated

30g fresh dill, finely chopped

2 tbs honey

2 lemons, juice of

150ml sunflower oil

Mix everything very well together. That's it!

The best coleslaw

Coleslaw is a classic example of something that is usually ok, if ordinary, but can be really excellent with just a couple of tweaks. The crucial bits are the relatively brief (but crucial) time the veg spends in the colander with salt and sugar; the addition of crème fraîche, vinegar and horseradish to the mayo; and the omission of onion.

I love the way that recipes are passed around and adapted. I ate this version (or something very like it) at Martin Orbach (of Shepherds Ice Cream)'s 60th birthday party as an accompaniment to pulled pork baps. That salad was actually made by Charlie Hicks, who used to do a food programme on Radio 4 and now brings the world of exotic vegetables to Herefordshire. And he got it (or something similar) from Felicity Cloake, who writes a column in *The Guardian* comparing lots of different versions of well-known dishes and then comes up with her version of the 'best of the best'.

Like most coleslaw this keeps well in the fridge for up to a week so you might as well make a decent-sized batch. It's the ideal accompaniment for pulled brisket (see page 227) as well as pulled pork (see page 231) and most other burgerish things.

Serves 12 generously – so make half or less if you don't want delicious leftover coleslaw in the fridge!

750g white cabbage, quartered, cored and very finely sliced

500g carrots, peeled and finely grated

10g salt

10g caster sugar

30ml white wine vinegar

120g mayonnaise (either Hellmann's or home-made – see page 244 but miss out the garlic)

60g crème fraîche

15g creamed horseradish

Mix the cabbage and carrots with the salt, sugar and vinegar. Put in a colander and leave in the sink to drain for an hour.

Mix everything together. Store covered in the fridge until needed.

Healthbowl

It all started with Dharmapala. Actually his name was Paul but when you were a macrobiotic chef in the early 1980s then 'Paul' simply didn't cut the mustard. Paul/Dharmapala used to make a delicious rice and lentil salad which he called a healthbowl. Early on at The Place Below, we developed our own version. Now we serve masses of it every day. It's relatively low in fat, has well-balanced plant-based protein and fresh vegetables (hence the name), and it's also very tasty.

Many different variations of the basic recipe are possible – add grated or cooked carrot, other fresh herbs, and almost any other vegetables you have to hand. Most can be stored in the fridge overnight, but blanched broccoli or halved cherry tomatoes must be eaten the day you make it. Try serving each portion on a sheet of toasted nori brushed with soy sauce – and if you like things a bit spicy add a few drops of tabasco to the dressing.

Serves 6 generously

300g sweet potato, peeled and diced

2 tbs sunflower oil

½ tsp salt

150g puy lentils

250g brown rice, long or short grain

For the dressing

1 piece stem ginger in syrup

60ml shoyu/goodquality soy sauce

60ml balsamic vinegar

20ml sesame oil, preferably cold pressed

40ml sunflower oil

1 tbs sesame seeds

1/2 head of celery, diced 1cm

200g closed-cap mushrooms, finely sliced

1 bunch fresh coriander or parsley, finely chopped

Toss the diced sweet potato in the salt and enough sunflower oil to coat it. Spread out on a baking sheet and roast at 180°C (fan) for 30-35 minutes until the sweet potato is quite tender and beginning to brown.

Cook the lentils in plenty of unsalted water for about 25 minutes until just tender. Drain well and put to one side.

Cook the rice in boiling water with a little salt (you need just over 1.5 times the volume of water to rice). As soon as the water returns to the boil, turn the heat right down and simmer, covered, until all the water is absorbed and the rice is cooked (about 30 minutes).

To make the dressing, in a blender, whizz together the stem ginger (without its syrup), shoyu, balsamic vinegar, sesame oil and sunflower oil, and then add the sesame seeds and stir into the puy lentils while they are still warm.

Allow the rice and the sweet potatoes to cool.

Add the remaining ingredients to the rice and sweet potatoes. Mix everything together thoroughly but gently, and serve. Like most salads it's nicer at room temperature than straight from the fridge.

Weekday family suppers

This chapter is not intended to be aimed exclusively at families – the title is simply a description of where the recipes and tactics have come from over the last 20 years of my life as our kids have been growing up. The recipes are easy to prepare without constant reference to detailed instructions, and they're dishes which are likely to produce uncontroversial pleasure.

In my own family the food pleasure that is uncontroversial has changed over time. My daughter Holly's prime delight as a five-year-old might have been a golden syrup pancake (no need to hold back on the golden syrup). These days after rowing training it's more likely to be a beef crumpet (page 255) or a home-made burger (page 139) that will bring her most enthusiastically to the table.

In general this chapter contains strategies rather than recipes, and there's a big overlap with my other favourite chapter – cooking with leftovers. So each of the recipes in this chapter are starting points from which to create reviving and simple weekday happiness. This is especially true of the two pasta recipes. We have probably eaten more pasta suppers than any other type of food over the last 20 years – and I'm sure that makes us entirely typical. But where does the idea of pasta take you? It takes me to see what's in the fridge and the cupboard, and then work out what goes with what.

Similarly the Spanish omelette – which could equally well be called a frittata – is born to be a vehicle for leftovers and unconsidered bits and pieces. Fairly random – but usually vaguely balanced – mixtures create truly delicious Spanish omelette suppers. Likewise, the recipe for burgers and their trimmings is a starting point for burger cooking rather than a recipe to be followed religiously. Feel free to make all sorts of alterations and additions.

Finally, the 'meal in a bowl' with chorizo and chickpeas is really a starting point for variations on the theme of 'pulses and pork', but without the chorizo, it can also be the basis of a delicious vegetarian dish.

If you're wondering if a particular ingredient (whether leftover or otherwise) will work just imagine yourself eating it – and your imagining tastebuds will probably give you a reasonably good idea of whether it will be good or not.

Burgers & their trimmings

We have high burger standards in Hereford these days as our city is home to two of the country's finest burger restaurants – The Beefy Boys and the truly exceptional Burger Shop run by A Rule of Tum.

This is not a situation for cleverness and originality but for doing simple things well. Take good mince, good bacon, good cheese and good buns and you're 80% of the way there – ideally 90% minced lean chuck steak mince to 10% hard beef fat. Other minces are also good: try the chorizo burgers on page 165 or mix lamb mince with garlic, chilli and mint.

Accompaniments to your burger are critical; try bacon, cheese, tomato and a bit of really sticky onion marmalade; I find Tracklements' onion marmalade especially good. Some may feel that sweet-pickled gherkins are an important extra. I like salad on the side rather than in the bun.

Brioche buns (see page 37) are currently fashionable homes for burgers and that's what I've used here, but squares of spianata (see page 31) are also excellent. Realistically for a weekday family supper your bun is likely to come from a bakery or your freezer – but still make sure it's a good one.

Serves 4

600g lean chuck steak, minced

60g hard beef fat, minced

2 tsp salt

¼ tsp freshly ground black pepper

4 buns – e.g. brioche buns

4 dsp onion marmalade

4 good-sized rashers streaky bacon, cut in half and fried until crisp

4 very thin slices melty cheese – cheddar, Gruyère or Emmental are all good

2 large tomatoes, thinly sliced – 2 slices per burger

Pre-heat the oven to 200°C (fan). Thoroughly mix the minced beef and fat with the salt and pepper and shape into 4 equal-sized burgers.

Heat a heavy cast-iron pan – I like the ridged kind that can go either on the hob or in the oven – brushed with a little sunflower oil. When it's hot put the burgers in and cook for 3 minutes on each side on a medium-high heat. Then transfer the pan to the pre-heated oven for about 6 minutes. Meanwhile halve the buns and spread the bottom with onion marmalade. When the 6 minutes are up put the burgers on top of the onioned bun, top with cheese, then tomato, then bacon, then a bit more cheese and put back in the oven, with the top of the bun by its side, for a further 3 minutes. The burgers should then be cooked right through – but check them with a probe (you're looking for 72° or above in the middle of the burger) or by eye to check that the meat in the middle is no longer pink.

Leave to rest for a couple of minutes in a warm place and then serve.

Chorizo, chickpeas & roast peppers
with tomato & smoked paprika

This is simple and delicious. Like all the recipes in this section it's a pointer rather than a set of iron-clad instructions and it can happily adapt to other vegetables such as aubergines or courgettes.

For a vegetarian version omit the chorizo and sprinkle either crumbled feta or grilled halloumi on each person's plate.

It's great with rice, couscous or good bread such as the spianata on page 31 or, for extra luxury, the home-made brioche (page 37) which is pictured here.

Serves 4

2 tbs olive oil (for the onion)
1 large onion, halved and sliced
500g cooking chorizo, chopped chunkily

2 red peppers
2 yellow peppers
2 tbs olive oil (for the peppers)
1 tsp salt

1 x 500g packet passata
1 tsp sweet smoked paprika
1 x 400g tin of chickpeas, including the water

optional: 30g flat leaf parsley, roughly chopped

Pre-heat the oven to 180°C (fan). Put the olive oil, the sliced onion and the chopped cooking chorizo in a casserole pan and cook with the lid on for about 15 minutes, stirring from time to time, until the onion is soft and the chorizo just cooked.

Toss the peppers with the second lot of olive oil and the salt. Spread on a large baking sheet and roast for 25-30 minutes until the peppers are browning at the edges and are quite soft. If you don't want to use the oven you could add the peppers at the same time as the onion and do the whole thing on the hob. It makes it quicker, but the peppers won't be as juicy and sweet that way.

Add the roast peppers, the passata, the smoked paprika and the chickpeas (with their water) to the chorizo mixture. Bring to the boil and simmer very slowly for 20 minutes or more. Check the seasoning – be wary of adding more salt as most chorizo is quite salty.

Garnish each bowlful with a generous scattering of chopped flat parsley – or not, as you prefer!

Sarah's smoked salmon pasta, & Our carbonara

In general I'm not a big fan of separate sauces with pasta – with the exception of a really good ragout – I'm rather looking for some piquant flavours and interesting textures, mixed in with the pasta before you serve it. Here we have two such recipes that are both very easy to make and delicious. Sarah's smoked salmon pasta is very quick, surprisingly rich, and a real favourite in my family, while the carbonara combines classic deliciousness with the essentially comforting blandness of the pasta.

Both dishes serve 4, based on 90g pasta per person (adjust according to appetite)

For both pasta dishes

350g pasta (preferably penne for the salmon, and de Cecco linguine for the carbonara)

For Sarah's salmon pasta

150g smoked salmon trimmings, roughly chopped

100ml double cream

200g fresh plum tomatoes, diced 1cm

2 good sized pak choy, about 250g, chopped in large pieces

15g fresh basil, roughly chopped/ torn

grated Parmesan and black pepper to serve (both optional)

For the carbonara

4 big rashers (about 150g) smoked streaky bacon, diced 1cm

150ml white wine

2 egg yolks mixed with a few drops of water to double-cream consistency

50g Parmesan

freshly ground black pepper

additional Parmesan to serve at table

For both pasta dishes

Put a large pan of salted water on to boil. When it's boiling add the pasta and bring back to a rolling boil. While it's cooking, warm some plates and make the accompanying sauce...whichever one you choose.

For Sarah's salmon pasta

In a large deep frying pan put the smoked salmon trimmings, the cream, the tomatoes and the pak choy. Bring to the boil and then turn off the heat. It doesn't need proper cooking. Stir in the basil.

When the pasta is cooked drain it and toss the drained pasta with the smoked salmon mixture. Serve at once with Parmesan and black pepper to add at the table.

For the carbonara

In a very large deep frying pan, fry the diced bacon in its own fat on a fairly high heat for 6 or 7 minutes until it's browning and the fat is running. Add the white wine and bubble fiercely until the wine has reduced by half. Keep on a very low heat until the pasta is cooked.

Drain the pasta (not too thoroughly). Toss the slightly damp pasta in the bacon and wine, stir well and then drizzle in the beaten egg yolks whilst stirring the pasta vigorously. Then quickly stir in the grated Parmesan. The residual heat of the pasta should be enough to just cook the egg yolks leaving a creamy coating.

Divide between warmed dishes, ensuring each person gets their fair share of bacon bits. Grind black pepper generously onto each plate.

Ham & pea risotto
(after gammon)

Risotto is one of our go-to family dishes and peas are one of our go-to family vegetables. Here's the two together packing a great big flavour punch. Cheddar feels a more natural accompaniment than Parmesan for these very British ingredients.

This is a dish I would only make after we've had gammon – there's no point trying to make it without gammon stock. Note: gammon stock is usually very salty so you're unlikely to need any extra salt in this recipe.

Serves 4

500ml smoked gammon stock (see page 225)

500ml cider

300g risotto rice

250g frozen peas

150g cooked smoked gammon, finely diced

25g butter

30g flat leaf parsley roughly chopped

70g strong cheddar, finely grated

Put the stock and cider in a pan and heat until just about boiling, then turn off the heat.

Put the risotto rice in another pan and place on a medium heat. Add the hot liquid a ladleful at a time over 15-20 minutes, stirring very regularly. Each ladleful should be more or less absorbed by the rice before you add the next one. When the rice is very nearly but not quite cooked, add the peas and the gammon and a little more stock and keep stirring. A couple of minutes later, when the rice is just cooked, stir in the butter, the parsley and half the cheddar, leaving the rest of the cheddar on the table for people to help themselves.

Chicken, leek & lemon risotto
(after roast chicken)

This is the most delicious and comforting dish to make from leftover roast chicken. As with the chicken and sweetcorn soup on page 63, don't bother making it unless you've got leftover roast chicken. Surprisingly it doesn't really matter how much meat you've left on the bird. It will be a richer dish with more chopped chicken stirred in but it's equally (although differently) good when it's closer to being a straightforward leek and lemon risotto.

Be sure to cook the leeks separately from the risotto. If you cook them in with the risotto you're almost certain to overcook them and overcooked leeks have an unattractive aroma.

Using a whole lemon makes this dish quite lemony. I really like that, but if you prefer your lemon a bit more retiring then just use half.

Serves 4 generously

1 litre chicken stock (see page 245)

300g risotto rice

400g leeks, halved, sliced 1cm, and thoroughly washed and drained

100ml white wine

50g butter

a couple of sprigs of fresh thyme, stripped

200g leftover roast chicken meat, chopped

1 lemon (zest and juice)

100g Parmesan (maybe less if you've got lots of chicken bits)

About half an hour before you're ready to eat, start cooking the risotto. Heat the stock to around boiling and keep it nearby.

Put the rice in a heavy-bottomed pan on a medium heat and stir it around for a couple of minutes. Then start adding the hot stock, stirring very regularly. As soon as one ladleful of stock is absorbed, add the next one.

While the risotto is beginning to cook, put the leeks in another lidded pan, with the white wine, butter and fresh thyme leaves. Cook on a very low heat with the lid on for five or more minutes until the leeks are barely tender. Add the chopped chicken and continue to warm gently until the chicken pieces are hot. Leave in a warm place.

When the rice is just cooked and the latest ladleful of liquid nearly all absorbed, add the leeks and chicken with their buttery/winey liquid and the juice and zest of the lemon. Check the seasoning and add salt and pepper as necessary. Stir well and then add half the grated Parmesan.

Serve at once – risotto doesn't like to be kept waiting. Offer the rest of the Parmesan at the table.

Spanish omelette, frittata, tortilla

The basic concept of a Spanish omelette, a frittata and a (Spanish) tortilla are all the same: interesting food (generally featuring potatoes and onions) mixed with beaten eggs and cooked in a pan until just set.

This approach is a stunning vehicle for leftovers. Onions and potatoes are always a good starting point but then add bits of chicken, ham, chorizo, roast peppers, courgettes, crumbly goats' cheese or feta (not melty cheese for my taste), peas, asparagus, parsley, thyme, rosemary – the list could go on and depends largely on what you've got in your fridge.

So the recipe below should simply be regarded as a starting point. Traditionally the potatoes would also be cooked directly in olive oil rather than boiled, but I find that boiling is easier and very satisfactory.

Serve with a simple green salad.

Serves 4 generously

500g large potatoes, halved (quartered if they're very large) and very thinly sliced

350g onions, quartered and thinly sliced

50ml olive oil

1 tsp salt (this will season the potatoes as well)

65g cooking chorizo (or smoked bacon) diced 1cm

1 red pepper, thinly sliced

1 yellow pepper thinly sliced

5 eggs, lightly beaten

75g feta cheese, crumbled

Bring a large pan of water to the boil and add the sliced potatoes. Bring back to the boil and simmer for 5 minutes until just cooked and drain.

Meanwhile put the onion, olive oil and salt in a very large deep frying pan and fry for 20-30 minutes until the onion is soft and sweet. Add the chorizo (or smoked bacon) and peppers and continue cooking for another 15 minutes until the chorizo is thoroughly cooked. Add the cooked potatoes and continue cooking for a couple of minutes so everything is piping hot and well mixed. Taste and check the seasoning; there is nothing duller than under-seasoned potato.

Lower the heat. Add the beaten eggs mixed with the crumbled feta and gently mix them into the other ingredients. Once everything is well mixed, allow to cook on a very low heat (as low as you can achieve) for about 10 minutes until the egg is cooked at the bottom of the pan but not at the top. Turn the grill on high and put the pan under the hot grill for 2-5 minutes (depending on the grill) until the top is set and lightly browned.

Allow the omelette to rest for a couple of minutes and then either serve direct from the pan or turn it out first onto to a big serving dish. It's best eaten warm rather than piping hot.

The simplest roast chicken dinner

When I'd just stopped being a vegetarian, everyone told me roast dinners were easy, but more or less refused to tell me how to do them. So for anyone who finds a lack of instruction in this area frustrating, here's my brief guide to the simplest possible (and very good) roast chicken. This recipe has recently been road-tested twice by my son Jonathan, so it genuinely is foolproof!

The key shortcuts compared with a classic roast chicken dinner are: no change of oven temperature; no need to make a separate gravy; no roast potatoes (but good boiled potatoes); no veg prep – just cook some frozen peas.

You'll need a roasting tin only slightly larger than the chicken. For larger or smaller chickens add/subtract 20 minutes per 500g above/below 1.75kg.

Serves 4 with plenty of leftovers

1 large free-range chicken, about 1.75kg

½ lemon

fistful of fresh rosemary and/or thyme left on the stalks

4 cloves garlic

salt – about 1 tsp

250ml white wine (red also works, as does cider)

200ml boiling water

1kg Charlotte potatoes

2 tbs olive oil

1 tsp salt

400g frozen peas

Pre-heat the oven to 170°C (fan). Remove the chicken from its packaging including any elastic bands around the legs. Check if there are giblets in the cavity – if there are, remove and put in the fridge ready to add to your next stockpot. Put half a lemon, some fresh thyme or rosemary and four halved but unpeeled garlic cloves in the cavity and give the lemon a quick squeeze into the cavity. Sprinkle the chicken skin with salt. Roast for about 30 minutes. Take it out and pour the wine and boiling water into the bottom of the roasting tray (not over the chicken). Put back in and roast for another 50 minutes to an hour until the internal temperature is at least 72°C (see above for timings for different sizes of chicken).

Meanwhile boil the potatoes 25-30 mins until just tender, drain, cut in half and toss with the olive oil and salt. Leave in a warm place.

When you think the chicken may be cooked, stick a digital thermometer probe into the deepest bit of meat (the inside of the thigh but not touching the bone) and ensure that the meat is at least 72°C. Leave it cooking for a few minutes more while you boil some frozen peas very briefly (not more than 3 minutes). Take the chicken out and serve, giving everyone generous amounts of winey cooking juices – no need to make gravy.

With luck and careful planning you'll have stock and chicken meat left over. Strip the meat off the bird and keep aside both meat and bones. See page 245 for how to make stock, and page 254 for using the chicken leftovers.

The 'not salad'

The concept of the 'not salad' came from my son Jonathan, who couldn't see the point of anything that involved a lot of leaves. If he ever showed signs of enjoying what I considered to be a salad he would tell me that in fact it wasn't a salad, it was a 'not salad'. In my mind this concept now covers all plates of food involving both raw and cooked ingredients – what might be called a 'salade composée' (plated salad) or a 'salade tiède' (warm salad).

Any number of ingredients could be included in this salad: leftover roast chicken/pork/beef; chilli/ginger/garlic; peppers/courgettes/tomatoes; asparagus/peas/beans; sausage/salami/chorizo; chickpeas/puy lentils; parsley/basil/dill; feta/goats' cheese/Roquefort. Just picture the combinations on the plate or in your mouth and see what your fridge offers. I'm usually looking for balance: some protein, some carbs, plenty of veg, strong flavours and varying textures. Frequently the dressing is created in the process of cooking the ingredients rather than made and added separately. It's tricky to make these for more than about 4 people at a time unless you have a truly large pan, as they're usually tossed together in the pan you've been cooking in.

Serves 2 generously or 4 modestly

150g good quality streaky bacon, diced 1cm

100g red onions, diced 1cm

2 tbs olive oil (for the bacon)

1 tsp salt

200g waxy potatoes, previously cooked and cooled (leftover baked potatoes would also work fine), diced 1cm

1 good head of broccoli (about 400g), in small florets with the tender part of the stem sliced very thinly

2 tbs balsamic vinegar

4 tbs olive oil

2 good–sized baby gem lettuces, torn into bite-sized pieces

100g fresh goats' cheese or feta, crumbled

In a large, deep frying pan fry the bacon and onions in the olive oil until the bacon is beginning to crisp and the onion is soft.

Add the diced cooked potatoes and the broccoli and cook on a medium-high heat for about 5 minutes until the broccoli is just tender.

Add the balsamic vinegar and stir thoroughly. Add the 4 tbs of olive oil and stir again. Then take off the heat and toss in the baby gem making sure the leaves are thoroughly coated with goo from the pan.

Divide between serving plates, putting leaves at the bottom and all the other bits, divided evenly, on top. Crown each plate with crumbled fresh goats' cheese and serve.

Friends for dinner

Cooking for and eating with friends is one of the great pleasures of life. For me, the preparation and the shopping are both very much part of that pleasure. So from buying asparagus or breast of lamb from our local farm shop, to snipping the crackling off the slow-cooked pork belly, to bringing the casserole of cider and rabbit to the table – it's all part of the enjoyment. I may be weird, but I even quite like washing up afterwards as long as there's nothing urgent to be done the next morning and there's some good music to listen to.

This chapter contains a selection of delicious recipes to feed friends when you're not too pushed for time and want to offer your pals something a little special or luxurious. Some of these dishes take a bit longer to make but none of them are difficult. The asparagus, ham and hollandaise has to be made at the last minute and is almost the only dish in the book with a slightly technical cooking skill (making hollandaise sauce). The mushroom and cep risotto is also done at the last minute, but for the others nearly all of the cooking can be done well in advance so you can spend more of your evening chatting with your friends.

One or two recipes require very long cooking times. Don't be afraid – give it a go. This method of long initial slow-cooking followed by a final quick blast in a hot oven evolved in the context of cafés and restaurants when you want to be able to produce a slow-cooked piece of pork belly within 15 minutes of the order coming in. But in the same way it works really well for feeding friends and family at home. You can do all the long slow bit well in advance and then whack the portioned meat and crackling back in the oven 15 minutes before you're ready to eat.

English cassoulet:
ham hock with haricot beans & sausages

A traditional French cassoulet is so rib-sticking that you can't move for about a week having had half a helping. This is a lighter version but with the same starting points: three different cuts of pork, some beans, and ultra-flavoursome cooking liquor. It has a higher proportion of vegetables than a traditional French cassoulet. For a slightly more dinner-party presentation you could top each portion with some thin slices of smoked duck breast.

Ideally and if I had no work to do afterwards, I would eat this with some very creamy mash and some simply boiled cabbage or spring greens. But for a lighter lunchtime dish at the cafés we tend to serve it with plain basmati rice and this also works well.

Serves 6

1 cured ham hock (bone in)

200ml dry cider (keep the rest for drinking with the meal)

1 bay leaf, broken

250g plain top-quality sausages, cut into 2cm pieces

100g smoked streaky bacon, diced

50ml olive oil

400g carrots, in big chunks

400g onion, in small dice

3 sticks celery, medium diced

2 cloves garlic, crushed

400g tin cooked haricot or cannellini beans

apple juice (optional)

½ lemon, juice of

1 tbs Dijon mustard

1 small bunch (about 40g) flat parsley, roughly chopped

Cook the ham hock with the cider and bay leaf and just enough water to cover. Bring to the boil and simmer gently for about 3 hours until tender. Keep checking the liquid levels as it's really easy for it to boil dry during a long cook. Keep the cooking liquor. Pull the meat off the bone, leaving it in fairly large chunks, and discard the bone.

In a separate pan, brown the pieces of sausage and remove. In the same pan, cook the diced bacon until it's browned, and then remove, leaving the fat in the pan. Into the pan, add the carrot, onion, celery and garlic and sweat for about 10 minutes with the lid on (don't add any salt to the vegetables as the cooking liquor from the cured ham hock will be rather salty). Then add the cooked haricot beans, the ham hock and its cooking liquor, the bacon and the sausages. Bring the whole thing to the boil and simmer gently for about half an hour.

At this point you will probably need to add some more water or apple juice in order that the dish is wet enough (it should be like a thick soup with chunks in) and not too salty.

Add the lemon juice, mustard and half the parsley. Check the seasoning and adjust, adding more lemon juice if necessary.

Sprinkle some more chopped parsley over each portion.

Pork belly, cider & great crackling

Pork belly, cider and salt: it's hard to imagine three other ingredients which can produce so much happiness. For an ultra rich and delicious plateful serve with Dauphinoise potatoes (page 239), but it's also really good with fresh spianata (page 31). Add some simple cabbage, runner beans or a green salad and you've got piggy perfection on a plate. You can also cook a whole belly (around 3kg) in one piece (serves 12), fitting it snugly into a large tray (30 x 40cm and 7cm deep). Give it longer to cook (4-6 hours) and increase the cider quantity proportionately.

Serves 4

1kg pork belly, bones still in
300ml cider
salt for sprinkling on the skin

Pre-heat the oven to 180°C (fan). Put the pork belly in a roasting tin, skin side up. Sprinkle a generous amount of salt over the rind. Roast for about 20 minutes until the top is beginning to brown.

Add the cider, cover the tray with foil and return to the oven for about 15 minutes, then turn the oven down to 120°C (fan) and leave for a further 3-4 hours. Check the liquid in the tin every hour or so and add boiling water if necessary. Liquids will evaporate much more quickly in a fan oven even when the roasting tray is carefully covered in foil. After about 3 hours the pork belly flesh should be collapsing – if it's still firm then leave it for longer.

When the meat is ready take it out of the oven. Remove from the tray and set aside. Skim the fat off the top of the liquid or use a gravy separator, and discard the fat. Reduce the remaining cidery juices over a gently heat, until you've got a bit less than half a litre of very tasty thin sauce. Season if necessary and leave on one side.

Meanwhile, using a large knife, carefully remove the (probably soggy-looking) crackling and use kitchen scissors to snip it into long thin strips. Put the thin pieces of crackling on a fresh roasting dish and put back in a very hot oven (200-220°C fan). After about 10 minutes, pour off any excess fat and continue roasting. Check every five minutes until it's nearly as crisp as you will want it – you'll return it to the oven for 5 minutes just before serving the pork.

Portion the pork into four pieces, following the line of the bones. About 15 minutes before you're ready to eat put the meat back in the oven at 180°C (fan). After about 10 minutes, put the crackling on top and put the cider juices back on the heat. In about five more minutes the whole lot will be ready to serve.

Rabbit in cider with mustard

Rabbit with mustard is a classic French combination. Adding cider is a natural thing to do if you live, as we do, in Herefordshire.

If you live in the country you'll feel a double joy at eating wild rabbit: it tastes delicious and there's too many of them. The two culinary challenges of eating rabbit are the small bones and the lack of fat. This recipe deals with the little bones by pre-cooking the rabbit whole and then taking the meat off the bones. And bacon and cream push the fat content up to acceptable levels.

If you're feeling particularly adventurous, and you can find an available supply, this dish also works well with squirrel.

Serve with either ordinary mash, celeriac and potato mash or, for a less rich meal, with basmati rice.

Serves 6 generously

2 rabbits, about 1.5kg in total

500ml dry cider or perry

a couple of sprigs of fresh thyme

1 bay leaf

1 tsp salt

300g thick-cut streaky bacon cut into strips

1 large onion, halved and sliced 1cm

400g carrots, halved and sliced 1cm

4 sticks of celery, sliced 2cm

2 tbs flour (about 20g)

100ml double cream

1 tbs Dijon mustard

Put the rabbit in a lidded casserole dish with the cider, thyme, bay leaves and salt. Bring to the boil and simmer either on a very low heat on the hob, or in a low oven 120°C (fan) for about 2 hours until the meat is tender. Take the meat out, allow to cool and reserve the cidery cooking juices, discarding the herbs. When the rabbit is cool enough to handle, strip the meat from the bones and tear into bite-sized chunks.

Using the same casserole dish, cook the bacon in its own fat until it's fairly crisp and plenty of fat has run out of it.

Add the onion and cook for about 5 minutes with the lid on; then add the carrot and celery and continue cooking with the lid on for another 10 minutes on a gentle heat. Then add the flour and cook whilst stirring for a couple of minutes.

Gradually add back the cidery cooking juices and the cream and bring to the boil, stirring all the time. Boil fiercely for a couple of minutes until the sauce has thickened slightly. Add the mustard and the cooked rabbit and continue to cook gently until the meat is thoroughly hot.

Check the seasoning and serve.

Breast of lamb with roast aubergine & peppers

We started eating breast of lamb at home following many conversations with Sarah's Aunt Kate, who is a regular and welcome guest and a great fund of cooking knowledge. Kate was brought up on breast of lamb and it has been a staple of her family cookery for many years. It's a flat shallow cut, fatty, tough and bony. But don't let that put you off – cooked overnight on a very low heat, it becomes tender and flavourful. This dish is best served warm rather than piping hot. Serve with plain rice, couscous or tabouleh (page 121).

Serves 4-6 depending on how hungry you are

1 breast of lamb, bone in (about 1.2kg, or equivalent in smaller pieces)

250ml red wine

250ml water/wine

2 medium aubergines (about 500g), diced 1cm

2 tbs olive oil (for the aubergine)

½ tsp salt

2 red peppers, in fat strips

1 tbs olive oil (for the peppers)

½ tsp salt

2 tbs olive oil

1 very large or 2 medium onions, quartered and thinly sliced

½ tsp salt

2 cloves garlic, crushed

1 tsp dried oregano

300g tomatoes – halved or diced 1cm

50g flat leaf parsley, roughly chopped

Put the breast of lamb in a lidded casserole dish and add the water and wine. Bring to the boil, put the lid on and put in a very low oven, around 120°C (fan), for 8-10 hours or overnight.

In the morning take the meat out of the oven, lift out of the liquid and put it on a plate to cool a bit. Separately let the liquid cool and then put in the fridge so that it's easy to take the hard fat off the top; this you can discard (lamb fat is no good for roasting potatoes), but reserve the cooking liquor.

When the lamb is cool enough to handle, take all the meat off the bone. This is best done with your hands as the meat comes in horizontal strips, and ideally you want to discard the solid fat, the bones and the shiny thin casing that covers each layer of meat. The meat should be in roughly bite-sized pieces. You will only get a small amount but it's exceptionally flavoursome. You can then leave the meat aside until you're ready to make the finished dish.

Toss the diced aubergine with the olive oil and salt and roast on a baking tray at 180°C (fan) for 30 minutes until very soft and browning at the edges. Repeat with the peppers, which will take only 25 minutes.

In the same dish you cooked the lamb in, fry the onion in the olive oil and salt for 20 to 30 minutes until very soft. Add the garlic and oregano, cook for 2 minutes, stir in the chopped tomato and cook for about 30 seconds. Take off the heat, stir in the roast aubergine and the peppers and the lamb. If the lamb has been in the fridge then warm the dish gently until the lamb is warm but not piping hot. Serve it straight away or re-warm later. Serve the cooking juices in a jug to pour over each plate.

Chorizo burgers
with slow-roast tomatoes & roast garlic mayo

We had a brief phase of serving a variety of very delicious burgers at the cafés. One of my favourites were these chorizo burgers – basically pork mince with chorizo spicing. They are good both chilli-hot (made with hot smoked paprika) or fragrant (made with sweet smoked paprika) or anywhere in between.

As with most burgers, the accompaniments are crucial. Slow-roast tomatoes (see below) and roast garlic mayo (see page 244) are both essential. Home-made brioche (see page 37) or ciabatta buns (page 25) complete the luxury. Serve with a simple green salad.

Note that the slow-roast tomatoes need starting a couple of hours before you need them – or you can roast them in advance. And the burgers are best mixed and shaped the day before you want to cook them.

The tomatoes are also lovely with toasted cheese or whizzed briefly for a pasta sauce.

Makes 6 x 160g burgers

For the burgers

900g pork mince (ideally two thirds pork shoulder and one third belly for a bit of extra fat)

10g salt

10g smoked paprika – hot or sweet, depending how you want the burgers

2 cloves garlic, crushed

1 tsp ground black pepper

50g fresh breadcrumbs

1 egg, lightly beaten

sunflower oil (for frying the burgers)

For the roast tomatoes

6 fresh plum tomatoes

2 tbs olive oil

½ tsp sugar

salt and pepper

Mix together all the burger ingredients except the sunflower oil, and form into burgers weighing 160g each or just over. Ideally leave them in the fridge overnight to mature.

Pre-heat the oven to 180°C (fan). Heat a little sunflower oil in a frying pan (ideally one that you can put in an oven as well). If you're cooking all six burgers at once you'll need quite a large flat-bottomed pan in order not to overcrowd them – or else use two pans.

When the oil is hot, carefully put the burgers in and cook on a medium heat for about 3 minutes on each side. Then transfer to the oven to finish cooking for a further 12 minutes. If you have a digital thermometer then you're looking for a 'well done' internal temperature of at least 72°C – you don't want to be eating undercooked pork mince. Once they're cooked the burgers can happily rest for a few minutes before serving.

Halve the plum tomatoes and put cut surface upwards in a roasting tray. Drizzle the olive oil on top and season with the sugar and salt and pepper. Cook in the oven at 140°C (fan) for a couple of hours until they look semi-dried.

Don't forget to serve with the roast garlic mayo on page 244!

Lownz's lamb tagine

Lownz has been our head chef at Michaelhouse for many years and I've never eaten anything he's made that is less than mouthwatering. He's a well-travelled chef and I think of this as his signature dish. The essence of it is the multi-layered flavour delivered by the vast array of spices. If you want to shorten the process you can buy the Ras el Hanout spice mix ready-made. Serve with either plain basmati rice or herby bulghur (page 243).

Serves 6

600g lamb shoulder, diced
2 tbs sunflower oil (for the lamb)
500g onions, diced 1cm
4 tbs olive oil (for the onion)
1 red chilli, finely chopped
4 cloves garlic, crushed
40g fresh ginger, peeled and chopped
2 tsp salt
1 dsp Ras el hanout, see page 247
1 tsp paprika
½ g saffron
½ tsp cayenne
2 green peppers, diced 2cm
1 x 500g packet passata
1 x 400g tin chickpeas, drained
500ml water
500g aubergine, diced 1cm
4tbs olive oil (for the aubergine)
1 tsp salt
30g flaked almonds, toasted
50g pitted dates, finely chopped
75g pitted olives, finely chopped
1 tbs honey
30g coriander, roughly chopped

In a large casserole dish brown the lamb in the sunflower oil in batches so that the pan isn't overcrowded. Set the meat to one side.

In the same casserole dish, fry the onions in the olive oil. When the onion is soft (about ten minutes) add the chilli, ginger, garlic and salt and continue cooking for about 5 minutes. Then add the Ras el hanout spice mix, paprika, saffron and cayenne and the diced green peppers. Cook for a couple of minutes more, stirring very regularly.

Add back the meat and the passata, water and chickpeas, bring to the boil, then turn the heat down to its lowest possible setting and simmer very gently for about 2 hours until the lamb is completely tender.

Meanwhile, pre-heat the oven to 180°C (fan). Toss the aubergines in the 4 tbs olive oil and salt, spread on a baking sheet and roast for about 30 minutes until golden brown and very tender.

When the meat is cooked add the olives, almonds, dates and aubergines. Cook on a very low heat for about 5 minutes on a low heat, stirring occasionally and gently.

Scatter a generous amount of chopped fresh coriander on each portion as you serve it.

Victoria's Vietnamese beef

This is adapted from a recipe from ex-Herefordian/Australian Victoria O'Neill (of *Cooking with Class*). I've never been to Vietnam so I've no idea if this is remotely authentic but I do know that the sweet aromatic spiciness is very good indeed. It's a regular on the café menus. There's quite a large proportion of vegetables in the casserole so you can serve it just with plain rice – it doesn't really need anything else.

Serves 6

1kg diced chuck steak
2 tbs sunflower oil
100ml dry sherry

4 cloves garlic, crushed
4cm knob of ginger, peeled and grated
1 tsp chilli flakes
2 tbs sunflower oil

1 large onion, diced 1cm
20g caster sugar
40ml soy sauce
1 tsp five-spice powder
75g tomato purée
1 tsp salt
½ tsp freshly ground black pepper
200ml water
400g carrots, sliced 1cm on the bias
½ head celery, sliced 1cm on the bias

30g fresh basil, roughly chopped
6 spring onions, chopped very small

In a large frying pan brown the meat in small batches and set aside. De-glaze the pan with the sherry and set aside.

In a large casserole dish fry the garlic, ginger and chilli flakes in the sunflower oil for a couple of minutes. Add the browned meat and sherry and stir very well, scraping the bottom of the pan to get any bits that have caught.

Add the onion, sugar, soy sauce, five-spice, tomato purée, salt, pepper and water. Bring to the boil, cover and simmer very gently for about 2 hours until the meat is nearly tender. Add the celery and carrots and continue cooking for a further 30 minutes until the meat is completely tender.

Stir in half the basil and spring onion and check the seasoning.

Sprinkle the remaining basil and spring onions as a garnish on each portion.

Lamb with puy lentils & lemon

This is adapted from a River Cottage recipe for lamb shanks and is very popular in our cafés. Lemon and orange balance beautifully with the slightly fatty lamb shoulder and the nutty lentils. Serve it with leeky mash (page 240) or herby bulghur (page 243).

Serves 6

200g puy lentils (or other speckled green lentils)

3 tbs olive oil
1 large onion, in small dice
3 sticks celery, 1cm dice
300g carrots, 1cm dice
4 cloves garlic, crushed
3 sprigs fresh thyme
2 tsp salt

2 tbs sunflower oil for the lamb
1kg diced lamb shoulder
400ml white wine

300g tomatoes, diced 1cm

2 lemons, juice and zest
1 orange, juice and zest
50g flat leaf parsley, roughly chopped

Boil the lentils in plenty of unsalted water for 25 minutes until just tender. Drain and put to one side.

Meanwhile, put the olive oil, onions, celery, carrots, garlic and thyme into a large casserole. Sweat on a medium heat with the salt for about 5 minutes and then turn off the heat.

In a separate pan, brown the lamb in the sunflower oil, in small batches so the pan is not over-crowded. Add the browned lamb to the vegetables. Add the wine to the pan you were browning the lamb in and boil fiercely for a couple of minutes whilst vigorously stirring all the tasty brown bits into it.

Then add this liquid to the vegetables and lamb together with the chopped tomatoes and the cooked and drained lentils.

Bring to the boil and simmer over a very low heat for about 1½ hours until the lamb is completely tender.

Add the juice and zest of the lemons and orange and half the parsley. Check the seasoning – it's surprising how much salt pulse-based dishes can require. Bring back to the boil and serve, garnishing each plate with some more parsley.

Asparagus, ham, new potatoes & lemon hollandaise

This is one of my desert island dishes. Spring on a plate. For preparing asparagus, snap the stems as near to the base as they will go and discard the bit that snaps off. No further trimming or peeling is required. If they bend instead, your asparagus is not fresh, and freshness is everything with asparagus. Which is why, in my view, eating asparagus out of season from far away countries is a waste of time and air miles. Don't be daunted by fear of the hollandaise. Making it by hand will produce the lightness and richness that you really want, and it's not complicated.

Serves 4

600g new potatoes e.g. Charlotte

2 tbs olive oil (for the potatoes)

salt and pepper

500g asparagus – about 7 medium spears per person

1 tbs olive oil (for the asparagus)

salt and pepper

For the hollandaise

2 egg yolks

1 dsp cold water

150g unsalted butter, melted and fairly hot

1 lemon, juice and zest

salt and pepper

250g best quality smoked ham, sliced

Boil the potatoes for about 25 minutes until just tender, drain them, halve them, toss in olive oil and season with salt and freshly ground black pepper. Put aside to keep warm.

Have your ingredients all prepared for the hollandaise before cooking the asparagus. Bring a large pan of water to the boil. When it's boiling add the prepared asparagus and bring back to the boil on a high heat. Depending on the thickness of the asparagus it can take from 30 seconds to about 3 minutes to be just tender. Keep testing by extracting a spear with some tongs and pressing the base between your fingers. When it's ready there should be a little give but not absolute softness. Drain the asparagus, toss in olive oil, season with salt and pepper and leave to keep warm.

Make the hollandaise. In a pan (not aluminium) put the egg yolks and a dessertspoonful of cold water. Whisk constantly and vigorously, whipping the pan on and off a low heat. The mixture will lighten and become frothy, then go creamy and pale. When the yolks are thick enough to retain the distinct marks of the whisk, remove from the heat and put on a stable surface (perhaps with a damp cloth underneath to add extra stability).

Continue whisking the egg yolks and begin to pour in the hot melted butter, slowly at first and then quicker as the sauce thickens. Then add the lemon juice and zest, half at a time. Season with salt and pepper and more lemon to taste. This is best served at once (you can keep the sauce warm for a bit but any attempt to re-warm it risks the sauce splitting).

Divide the ham, potatoes and asparagus between warmed plates and then put a generous ladleful of hollandaise over each portion of asparagus.

Field mushroom & cep risotto

There are many mushroom risotto recipes out there. This one is on the beefy rather than the creamy end of the taste spectrum. This is curious as it's vegetarian. Indeed prior to the final addition of butter and Parmesan (neither of which are essential) it's vegan. It's a fairly easy dish to cook in large quantities as long as you've a big enough pan – and as long as you don't try to leave it to cook whilst you go and do something else. Risotto needs frequent stirring.

Dried ceps (also known as porcini mushrooms, Penny Buns or Boletus Edulis) are glorious both to eat and to sniff in their packet. They are great for risotto, and for mushroom sauces (see page 245) and for adding to beef dishes of many kinds (see for instance the beef and ale pie on page 89). The flavour comes at least as much from the soaking liquor as from the rehydrated mushrooms themselves. Serve with a sharply dressed green salad.

Serves 4 generously

50g dried ceps
350ml hot water
350ml red wine
1 tbs soy sauce (more to taste)

50ml olive oil
500g onions (2 large ones), halved and sliced (to give half rings)
2 cloves garlic, crushed
salt
750g field mushrooms, thickly sliced

250g risotto rice

50g butter
100g freshly grated Parmesan

Soak the ceps in the hot water for about half an hour. Pick out the rehydrated ceps and set on one side. Pour the liquid through a fine sieve into a pan, trying to leave any grit at the bottom of the bowl. Add the red wine and soy sauce, bring to the boil and switch off.

In a large heavy-bottomed pan, heat the oil. Add the onions and cook over a medium heat. After about five minutes add the crushed garlic and a little salt. Continue cooking for at least another 10 minutes until the onion is very tender. Turn up the heat and add the field mushrooms. If you don't have a very large pan you may have to add the mushrooms a few at a time, stirring regularly.

Once the mushrooms have collapsed in size and begun giving off their juices, add the rice and stir for a couple of minutes. Turn the heat down to medium, add the rehydrated ceps and begin adding the hot wine mixture. Add the first ladleful and stir vigorously. Once this is largely absorbed, add some more and continue this process until you have used up all the liquid. At this point the rice will probably not be quite cooked, so have a ready-boiled kettle at hand to add a bit more liquid. Continue cooking until the rice is just cooked and there is a little liquid left in the pan – it should be only slightly more solid than soup. Keep checking the risotto as it will easily burn, and keep tasting the rice to see when it is ready.

Once the rice is cooked, stir in the butter and grated Parmesan and serve at once.

Leek & Gruyère brioches

with white wine & tarragon sauce

This is a pretty, somewhat rich and very delicious vegetarian dish – a good example of the kind of thing which should appear on smart restaurant menus but generally doesn't. If you make the brioche yourself then it all takes quite a long time, but as long as you make enough brioche dough, you'll have the treat of fresh brioche for breakfast. You can of course use bought brioches but they may not be quite as good.

Serve the stuffed brioche with the white wine and tarragon sauce, some new potatoes and perhaps purple sprouting or asparagus in season or ordinary broccoli at other times.

Serves 4

25g butter

400g leeks, trimmed, halved and in 2 cm slices

2 tsp wholegrain mustard

80g Gruyère, grated

70g plain Greek yoghurt

salt and pepper

4 individual brioches (see recipe on page 37)

For the sauce

10g butter

½ small carrot, very finely diced

¼ medium red onion, very finely diced

½ stick celery, very finely diced

¼ tsp salt

½ tsp dried tarragon

175ml white wine

cooking juices from the leek filling

175ml double cream

Pre-heat the oven to 160°C (fan). Sweat the leeks in the butter with a little salt until quite tender. Drain very well, reserving any cooking juices. Mix with the mustard, Gruyère, yoghurt and seasoning, keeping a little of the cheese separate.

Cut off the tops of the brioches. With a small knife, cut around the middles of the brioches and pull out the insides, trying to get as close to the sides and bottoms as you can without making any holes (don't throw away the insides as they are fantastic for bread and butter pudding or posh breadcrumbs). Stuff them as full as you can with the filling, piling it a bit beyond the top. Scatter the remaining cheese on the stuffed brioches and leave the lids off.

Put them on a baking sheet in the pre-heated oven for 15-20 minutes. They are ready when they are heated right through and the bits of filling are just beginning to colour. Put the lids on 5 minutes before the end of the cooking time so they can warm through.

For the sauce

On a low heat melt the butter and sweat the finely diced carrots, onion and celery with a little salt and the dried tarragon for about 10 minutes until they are tender and giving off a little liquid.

Add the white wine and any leek stock left over from the filling. Bring to the boil and boil fiercely, uncovered, for about 5 minutes to reduce the volume by about a quarter.

Add the cream and bring back to the boil. Simmer until the sauce is the consistency of pouring cream. Take off the heat and season to taste with salt and pepper, ready to serve with the brioches.

Three-mushroom tartlet with cep sauce

This is one of a small number of recipes re-written from my previous two cookbooks. It's a great example of a fantastically flavoursome, satisfying and beautiful vegan dish in a smart dinner party style. You can use various wild mushrooms – pieds de mouton are especially good. I have specified the three varieties below because they taste wonderful, and because they are all cultivated and therefore relatively easy to get hold of.

The tartlet cases, the pine-nut purée and the cep sauce can be made the day before but the tartlets should not be put together until just before they're heated or they will go soggy. In this photo I've served the tartlet with the cep sauce, savoy cabbage and roast parsnips. If you're really hungry you could add some mash, with or without celeriac.

Serves 4

For the tartlet

You'll need 4 individual tartlet tins

250g wholemeal pastry (see page 67) using only vegan margarine, not butter

4 cloves garlic with skin on

40g pine nuts, lightly toasted

1 tbs lemon juice

35ml water

1 sprig fresh thyme, stripped

¼ tsp salt

175g field mushrooms, cut into large chunks

175g oyster mushrooms

175g shitake mushrooms

2 tbs sunflower oil

good pinch of salt for each batch of mushrooms

For the cep sauce

See recipe on page 245

Pre-heat the oven to 160°C (fan). Roll out the pastry very thinly and line the tartlet tins. Be careful not to stretch it or it will shrink while cooking. In each tin, use baking beans or an identical tin to weight the pastry so that it doesn't puff up while baking. Bake for 15-20 minutes until the pastry is just cooked and beginning to brown.

Spread the garlic cloves out on a baking sheet and roast in the oven for about 20 minutes until they smell nutty and are a little soft when prodded. Allow them to cool and then peel them.

Put the peeled baked garlic in a blender with the toasted pine nuts, lemon juice, water, fresh thyme and salt. Whizz until smooth and then taste. You need it quite assertive as it goes on in a thin layer. Adjust the seasoning with extra lemon juice or salt as necessary.

Next fry the mushrooms in the oil, in small batches on a high heat, seasoning each batch as you go. If you fry too many at once or over too low a heat, they will sweat and go slimy – you want them slightly browned and tender. Keep the pan fairly dry as you fry.

When all the mushrooms are fried you are ready to assemble the tarts. Do this just before you're going to heat them up. Divide the pine-nut mixture between the blind-baked tartlet cases and spread it evenly over each one. Arrange the fried mushrooms on top, starting with the field mushrooms, then the oyster mushrooms and lastly the shitake mushrooms arranged bottom up.

Before serving, pre-heat the oven to 160°C (fan) and heat the tartlets on a baking sheet for about 15 minutes until piping hot.

Puddings & tarts

Cakes, cookies and flapjacks may be delightful distractions, but puddings and tarts are events in themselves. Something to gladden and comfort us, usually at the end of a meal – although crumble for breakfast is no bad thing.

Sarah and I have recently (rather to my surprise) become enthusiastic Masterchef watchers. Whilst I'm full of admiration for some of the evident technical skills, I find that fairly frequently the complexity of their plates distracts from the main elements of deliciousness. So personally I would prefer a perfectly made lemon tart (crumbly pastry, silky smooth lemon filling with a real hit of lemon) with a blob of Charlie's crème fraîche from Neal's Yard creamery just up the hill from us, than a clever dish of lemon served seven ways where, even if the lemon curd is perfect, there's only a smear on the plate that barely gets your tastebuds going before you're asked to move on to granita and soufflé and candied peel and foam and boiled lemon sweets and… is your head exploding yet?

I'm generally not a big fan of creamy puddings, but I do make an exception for the meringue recipe given here. It's essentially an up-market pavlova with small but crucial differences. The passion fruit cream is delicious as a pud on its own – maybe with a bit of lemon shortbread (see page 197). But the combination of passion fruit and ripe mango is pure heaven. This and the chocolate, chilli and rosemary pot are naturally both attractive and seductive. And whilst the crumble is not groundbreaking, it is classically tasty and gently comforting.

At the cafés we're always looking for great ways of showing off seasonal fruit, and the tart recipes on page 189 do this really beautifully.

If I had to choose just one tart to have each day for the rest of my life, it would certainly be a lemon tart. But which of the three on page 191? Tricky.

Apple & raspberry crumble

Crumbles of all descriptions are for me the desert island dessert. If all other puddings (including chocolate cake, lemon tart and sticky toffee pudding) were taken away I could live a happy puddingful existence with just crumble. I think at least 50% of the puddings I had as a child were crumbles and they were always good.

Just think of all the possibilities: plum, peach, rhubarb, gooseberry, pear and raspberry, apple and pear, damson, greengage, even strawberry (surprisingly) and then there's the infinite variety of toppings. There's no right and wrong in the world of crumble but this is my current favourite on the topping front (courtesy of Dean at All Saints). The toasted hazelnuts and oats add both texture and richness of flavour.

This recipe probably can't be described as cutting-edge, but it is very good and surely we all need a reliably delicious crumble recipe to hand at all times?

If you're able to make the crumble topping the day before, or even a couple of hours before, and then refrigerate it before assembling the dish, this gives an even nicer texture to the crumble. Not essential, but good.

Serves 6-8

For the fruit

800g Bramley apples, cored, peeled and cut into chunks

1 tbs water

½ tsp cinnamon

75g sugar

300g raspberries – fresh or frozen

For the crumble

75g wholemeal flour

50g rolled oats

75g hazelnuts, toasted & semi-whizzed so they are somewhat chopped

½ tsp cinnamon

75g light muscovado sugar

75g butter

For the fruit

Put all the fruit ingredients except the raspberries in a pan together and heat gently with the lid on, stirring occasionally until the apple is mushy (unless you are one of the sad people who prefer Bramleys still in firm chunks, in which case cook it a bit less). Take off the heat and stir in the raspberries.

For the crumble

Whizz the topping ingredients together in a food processor until it resembles breadcrumbs with perhaps the odd bigger clump.

Pour the fruit into a crumble dish. Spread the crumble mixture on the top, and bake for 40 mins at 160°C (fan) until the top of the crumble is brown and the fruit is bubbling.

Passion fruit & mango meringue

This is the obvious dish to have for dinner when you've had hollandaise sauce earlier in the meal, since you've got those egg whites left over. So the ultimate April/May meal for me is asparagus, new potatoes, smoked ham and lemon hollandaise, followed by passion fruit and mango meringue for pudding. If you can get Alfonso mangoes in season then you're doubly lucky. Look out for passion fruit with very wrinkled skin as this is the sign of ripeness – you can often find them in this state in the 'reduced' section of supermarkets.

I find it challenging to serve large meringues – I always end up with a big mess. Doing the meringues individually means you can make each one lovely – if chunks of mango start sliding off the cream they still look and taste beautiful!

You can use caster sugar instead of light muscovado for the meringues and it certainly makes the whisking of the meringue quicker, but I really like the slight toffee-ish taste that you get from the light muscovado. Meringues are most easily made with a stand-mixer like a Kenwood Chef or a Kitchen Aid, but a handheld electric whisk is also fine if you have the patience to stand whisking for quite a few minutes.

Serves 4-5

For the meringue

100g light muscovado sugar

2 egg whites (approx. 80g)

For the fruit cream

4 ripe passion fruit

2 tbs caster sugar

200ml double whipping cream

For the topping

3 ripe mangoes (Alfonso if possible; fewer if they are larger than Alfonsos)

With your hands in the sugar, massage out any big lumps (muscovado sugar has a tendency to go lumpy). Pre-heat the oven to 110°C (fan).

Whisk the egg whites. After about 30 seconds, once the whites are looking somewhat fluffy but still fairly wet, start adding the sugar whilst continuing to whisk. Once all the sugar has been added, continue whisking until the egg whites are forming stiff peaks. This can take as long as 10 minutes using light muscovado sugar.

Line a couple of large baking sheets with greaseproof paper or re-useable baking mats. Using a large serving spoon, dollop the meringue mix into four or five large blobs and then, using the back of the spoon, make them into flattish round discs about 10cm diameter. Bake for 2½ -3 hours until the meringues are crisp on the outside but still a bit chewy in the middle. Leave to cool.

Scoop the pulp from the passion fruit, add the caster sugar and blitz briefly to break up the clumps of fruit. Whip the cream to soft peaks and gently fold in the sweetened passion fruit. Peel the mango and cut into long chunks, which give a feeling of generosity.

To serve, put a meringue on a plate, pile a good dollop of passion fruit cream on it, and then arrange its share of mango pieces on top.

Chocolate pots with chilli & rosemary

Chocolate and rosemary pots are an old favourite of mine. I've recently tried adding a little chilli to the mix and I think it's absolutely stunning. The chilli quantity given below provides gentle warmth – feel free to increase it if you're looking for a more blow-your-head-off type of experience.

If you've never tried the chilli/chocolate combo before, give it a go – it takes chocolate to a new and good part of the taste spectrum. Don't be tempted to substitute fresh chillies – the dried chilli flakes give the right degree of control for this recipe.

Serves 6

½ lemon, juice of

200ml white wine

25g caster sugar

600ml double cream

2 sprigs fresh rosemary

½ tsp chilli flakes

250g dark chocolate, broken into chunks

Warm the lemon juice, wine and sugar in a steel saucepan until the sugar has dissolved. Stir in the cream; the mixture will thicken. Add the rosemary, chilli flakes and chocolate and stir until the chocolate has melted.

Bring to the boil. Turn down and simmer very gently stirring every few minutes for about 30 minutes until the mixture is dark and thick (if the mixture separates, allow to cool and whizz it with a stick blender).

Leave to cool for about 5 minutes and strain into a jug; then pour into six ramekins or small coffee cups. Allow to cool for several hours in the fridge until set.

Prune & cider tart
Pear & raspberry tart
Rhubarb & almond tart

Three fruit tarts

Prune & cider / Pear & raspberry / Rhubarb & almond

These three tarts are all variations on frangipane tarts. This is a great approach for all kinds of different seasonal fruit – as well as non-seasonal things like prunes. Glazing the tarts makes all the difference to their attractiveness.

The possible variations are endless and include nectarines, gooseberries, plums, greengages and figs. I've given below three of my favourites. Cooking times vary with the fruit – especially its wetness. The prune and rhubarb tarts both take about 30 minutes (as long as the rhubarb is cooked dryly as described). The pear and raspberry takes closer to 45 minutes if the pears are juicy and ripe.

Prune and cider: 150g pitted prunes, soaked overnight in 40ml cider. Incorporate any un-soaked-up cider into the frangipane mixture.

Pear and raspberry: 2 small pears, peeled, cored and sliced, and a handful of raspberries. If the pears are ripe they don't need pre-cooking; if they are hard, pre-roast the slices in a little butter, lemon juice and sugar until barely tender.

Rhubarb and almond: 250g rhubarb in 2cm chunks, tossed with 35g caster sugar and pre-baked at 140°C (fan) for an hour until barely tender.

Makes 1 x 23cm tart, serves 6-8

1 x sweet pastry case (see page 251) blind-baked

85g butter

85g caster sugar

2 eggs

70g ground almonds

prepared fruit – see above

35g apricot jam (or redcurrant jelly for red fruit tarts)

1 tbs water

Cream together the butter, sugar, eggs and ground almonds, using a food processor, until pale. Spread the almond mixture on the pre-baked tart. Arrange the fruit on top.

Bake at 150°C (fan) for 30-45 minutes or until just set and light golden brown. To test if the centre is cooked, insert a sharp knife into a non-fruity bit. If it comes out cleanly the tart is cooked. Leave to cool.

Make the glaze by heating the jam and water together over a low heat and then mixing well to give an easy-to-spread consistency. Use a pastry brush to brush the glaze evenly over the tart when it is cool (if the tart is still warm the glaze will soak into the frangipane mixture).

Lemon curd tart
Treacle, honey
& lemon tart
Lemon & almond tart

Three lemon tarts:
Treacle, honey & lemon / Lemon & almond / Lemon curd

For each of these tarts (three of my favourites), start with a 23cm blind-baked sweet pastry case. Note: for the lemon curd tart, blind bake the tart shell for an additional 5 minutes, as it gets very little further cooking.

Serves 6-8

Treacle, honey and lemon tart

250g golden syrup

200g honey (if using set honey, melt it first)

1 lemon, juice and zest

30g butter, melted

150g white breadcrumbs

Lemon and almond tart

2 eggs

150g icing sugar

90g butter, melted and cooled

100g ground almonds

2 lemons, juice and zest

1 dsp flaked almonds to garnish

Lemon curd tart

100g butter

200g caster sugar

3 lemons, zest and juice

4 eggs, lightly beaten

Treacle, honey and lemon tart

Mix all the ingredients together thoroughly and pour into the blind-baked tart case.

Bake at 150°C (fan) for 35-45 minutes until ready to set. Look for a risen slightly golden brown surface to the filling. Allow to cool thoroughly before serving – this tart won't actually set until cooled.

Lemon and almond tart

Whisk the eggs and icing sugar until the mixture is very pale, much lighter in texture, and triple or more its original volume.

Whisk in the melted cooled butter – keep whisking as you slowly trickle in the butter (to avoid the mixture curdling). Fold in the ground almonds with a large metal spoon and a brisk cutting motion. When they're just incorporated fold in the lemon juice and zest in the same way, and sprinkle with the flaked almonds. Bake at 150°C (fan) for 30 minutes until just set.

Lemon curd tart

Pre-heat the oven to 150°C (fan). Put the lemon zest, lemon juice, butter and sugar in a saucepan and heat over a low heat until the sugar has all melted.

Stir the lightly beaten eggs into the butter and lemon syrup mixture. Cook over a lowish heat and stir continuously with a wooden spoon to make sure it doesn't scramble. Continue until the mixture coats the back of a wooden spoon. Immediately take it off the heat. If your mixture is scrambled or at all lumpy, whizz it with a handheld blender – smoothness is everything with lemon curd. Pour it evenly into the blind-baked tart shell and bake for 10-15 minutes until just set. Allow to cool before eating.

Cakes (& cookies & traybakes)

Not all of us can get through the day from one meal to the next without a little calorific restoration. So cookies, brownies and the like are the bedrock of all great cafés. Offer me a salted caramel brownie and a well-made flat white and my morning suddenly improves. This chapter homes in on these delicious moments.

We're just coming towards the end of what are probably peak cake-eating years at home. Jonathan and Holly are 18 and 14 respectively and have for the last few years made it clear that they felt the Sewell household should always provide cake or cookies or similar, to deal with the first pangs of post-school hunger. Probably brownies have been the most frequent fuel, and of those the salted caramel brownies on page 203 are currently the family favourites. The sticky lemon cake has made many appearances as a birthday cake and the chocolate chip cookies get consumed with enormous speed when they're available (by me as well as the kids). But honourable mention must also go to Hugh Fearnley-Whittingstall's banana bread (from the *River Cottage Family Cookbook)*, which I was tempted to include as Sarah has made it at home so frequently and to such acclaim from the rest of us – but since I don't really have anything new to say about it, I'll just direct you to the original source!

Of the cakes that we serve at the cafés, our sumptuous carrot cake is probably the most popular. We also like to serve cakes that we can use with whatever fruit is in season, and the New York Times torte, the streusel cake and (surprisingly) the sticky lemon cake work well as carriers of a wide variety of British fruit.

And talking of seasonal fare, I've included my favourite mince pie recipe. One Christmas I ran out of home-made mincemeat, and baked the last few (for us at home) with a jar of shop-bought mincemeat that had been in the larder for a while. Jonathan thought it tasted a bit alcoholic and it turned out to have a 'use by' date of 1995 – three years before he was born. I must go through all those old jars at some point…

Also slipped into this chapter are Edna's cheesy biscuits. We most often eat them at village celebrations with a glass of wine or cider, but they're also fabulous to fill a moment of savoury daytime hunger.

May your biscuit and cake tins be forever full!

Chocolate chip cookies

There is a recipe for chocolate chip cookies in my first cookbook but my taste has evolved over time. This recipe, based on one from expert in classic USA cooking, Martha Stewart, is just as buttery and chocolatey as my earlier recipe but a touch less sweet and all the better for that. I'm always suspicious when recipes are described as 'quick and easy' but this is genuinely quick, easy and exceptionally delicious.

These are now a daily delight in both my cafés.

Makes 30 cookies

250g softened butter

300g light muscovado sugar

2 eggs, lightly beaten together

1 tsp vanilla essence

325g plain white flour

1 tsp salt (less if you're using salted butter)

½ tsp baking powder

350g good-quality dark chocolate chips

Pre-heat the oven to 180°C (fan).

Butter and line with baking parchment two very large (or several smaller) baking sheets.

Cream the butter and sugar in a food processor until pale brown and fluffy.

Add half the beaten egg and the vanilla essence. Whizz until incorporated and then repeat with the rest of the egg, the plain flour, the salt and the baking powder and whizz for as a short a period as necessary to mix it all properly together.

Add the chocolate chips and pulse briefly to distribute them through the mixture.

Using two desertspoons, put blobs of the mixture onto the baking sheets. Each blob should weigh about 40g to make an even batch that Paul Hollywood might approve of, but no harm will be done by creating a variety of sizes. You need to leave big gaps around each blob as the cookies will expand as they bake.

Bake at 180°C (fan) for 10-14 minutes until brown at the edges.

Remove from the oven and leave the cookies to cool on the baking sheets for a couple of minutes. Then transfer to cool fully on a wire rack. When completely cool, store them in an airtight jar. But they're best eaten within a day or two of baking.

Perfect lemon shortbread

I'm a recent convert to shortbread. It's such a simple thing and yet, a bit like a tomato salad, it can be either a thing of exciting beauty or something dull and pointless. This recipe, adapted from Felicity Cloake's excellent *Guardian* column, is buttery, delicate and crumbly – and extremely moreish. I love the lemon flavour in this, but if you prefer it plain then just leave out the lemon zest.

To ensure that your shortbread is always perfect, use plain flour, not a strong white bread flour, and make sure the butter is really soft before beating it with the sugar. Don't be tempted to omit the ground rice – it adds a delicious nubbly texture which is perfect for shortbread. Be careful not to overwork the dough, and make sure you leave time to chill the biscuits before baking.

These are at their most spectacularly delicious when still slightly warm.

Makes about 22 biscuits

250g butter

125g caster sugar

285g plain flour

90g ground rice

2 lemons – finely grated zest only

extra caster sugar for sprinkling on after baking

Pre-heat the oven to 130°C (fan). Grease and line two 30cm x 40cm baking sheets or the equivalent.

Put the very soft butter and the caster sugar into a large mixing bowl, and beat with a handheld electric mixer until very soft and fluffy.

Add the flour, ground rice and lemon zest and mix swiftly with a large spoon so it is beginning to come together. Then use your hands to pull it together into one blob.

Roll the dough out to ½cm thick and cut out rounds with a 7cm-diameter cookie cutter. Do not use extra flour when rolling out the dough. Re-use leftover dough until it's all used. Put cookies onto baking sheets leaving a little space in between each one. Refrigerate for 30 mins before baking.

Bake for 50 minutes until cooked but not brown. Leave on the tray for 2 minutes and then transfer to a cooling rack and sprinkle with caster sugar. I find that sifting the caster sugar through a tea strainer makes it easier to do an even coating. Once cool, the shortbread can be stored in tins with baking parchment between layers.

Edna's cheesy biscuits

These biscuits are the toast of West Herefordshire, but do they originate with our neighbour Angela's mother's cook, or was it Edna, Audrey or Pat? In our village we call them Edna's cheesy biscuits (although Edna is sadly no longer with us), and they enliven most village events. Shaun Hill, now of the wonderful Walnut Tree Inn near Abergavenny, makes a very similar biscuit but with blue cheese and topped with sesame seeds. Also delicious.

Makes 20-40 biscuits, depending on the size

225g grated cheddar (or mix of cheddar and Parmesan)

150g butter/margarine

150g self raising flour

½ tsp mustard powder

¼ tsp cayenne pepper

Paprika, fennel seeds, or sesame seeds to decorate

Put everything except the paprika and the seeds in the whizzer and whiz until it comes together. Roll into walnut-sized spheres and place on a tray lined with baking parchment. When the tray is full press a fork dipped in cold water onto each ball to flatten and decorate.

Sprinkle on the top (if you like) a little paprika, some sesame seeds or fennel seeds.

Bake at 180°C (fan) for 10-12 minutes until golden brown. They burn easily so watch them carefully. Leave on the trays for about 10 minutes before transferring to wire racks to cool.

Chocolate & chestnut cake

Chocolate and chestnut is a classic combination. We started making a Hugh Fearnley-Whittingstall recipe a few years ago and have simplified and adapted it to produce what is one of my favourite cakes. Rich but not cloying, light but intense – and it's gluten-free.

Chestnut purée is not invariably available in supermarkets, but you can buy it throughout the year direct from Merchant Gourmet's website if you can't find it closer to hand.

This cake regularly features on our Christmas menus. I like to eat it with a blob of crème fraîche.

Serves 8

200g chocolate (70% cocoa solids is best for this)

200g butter

In a large pan, melt chocolate and butter together over a low heat.

100g chestnut purée

40ml milk

In a separate pan, or in the microwave, warm the chestnut purée and milk. Stir to mix thoroughly together so you have a smooth paste. Mix this into the chocolate/butter mixture.

3 eggs, yolks and whites separated

100g caster sugar

Mix egg yolks with caster sugar and then stir this into the chocolate mixture.

Whisk egg whites until they form stiff peaks, then fold carefully into the chocolate batter.

Pour into a greased lined 20cm springform tin or silicone mould.

Bake at 150°C (fan) for about 50 minutes until just set. Allow to cool before carefully removing from the tin/mould.

Luxurious salted caramel chocolate & walnut brownies

This is a seriously luxurious brownie which I like to eat in smallish pieces accompanied by strong coffee. The recipe is derived from multiple sources, but primarily from Bakers, a famous New York bakery. It uses 70% chocolate to balance the sweetness of the caramel.

You can buy condensed milk and make your own caramel, but it's very much easier to buy the pre-cooked Carnation caramel. I think this is a perfectly balanced brownie, but if you like it very caramelly then use 2 tins of caramel and 2 teaspoons of salt.

I've also made this recipe with gluten-free white bread flour (Doves' Farm) in place of the plain flour and it's equally delicious.

Makes 32 small but rich brownies

375g dark chocolate (70% cocoa solids), broken into rough chunks

325g butter

500g light muscovado sugar

6 eggs, lightly beaten

1 tsp vanilla essence

200g plain flour or Dove's gluten-free bread flour

25g cocoa powder, sieved to remove lumps

½ tsp salt

200g walnuts, roughly chopped and toasted

1 x 397g tin Carnation caramel

1 tsp salt

Grease and line a baking tray 25cm x 35cm or equivalent. Pre-heat the oven to 160°C (fan).

In a large pan melt the chocolate and butter together over a low heat for 3-5 minutes, stirring regularly until they are both completely melted and amalgamated. Break up any lumps in the sugar, mix it in and allow the mixture to cool to room temperature.

Once the chocolate mixture is cool, mix in the eggs and vanilla extract, a small amount at a time, mixing as little as possible.

Gently stir in the flour, cocoa powder and salt – again mixing as little as necessary. Finally, briefly stir in the toasted walnut pieces and pour the whole mixture into the prepared tin.

Beat the salt into the caramel to loosen it up a bit. Then spread the caramel all over the top of the uncooked brownie mix. Use a knife or spatula to swirl the brownie and caramel mixes together. Don't worry about too much prettiness as you probably won't be able to see a beautiful pattern after it's baked.

Bake for about 40 minutes until slightly crusty on top and just set.

Allow to cool before cutting and serving.

Sticky lemon cake with blueberries

This sticky lemon cake has been on our menu for well over 20 years. I'm normally a great believer in leaving well alone – if a recipe is delicious then don't tinker with it. But earlier this year Lou, our Cambridge baker, made a version with fresh blueberries and I thought it was stunningly good. Blueberries can be a bit bland, but their juiciness paired with the sweet tartness of the lemon cake and syrup is perfect. For a more full-on combination I've also enjoyed this cake with rhubarb (pre-cooked as for the rhubarb and almond tart on page 189) in place of the blueberries. Use 100g rhubarb (cooked weight) for this.

Makes 12 modest pieces

125g butter, softened
175g caster sugar
2 eggs, lightly beaten together
175g plain flour
2 tsp baking powder
1 lemons, juice and zest

75g fresh blueberries

1 lemon, juice and zest
90g icing sugar

Pre-heat the oven to 140°C.

Grease and line a 20cm x 30cm x 5cm baking tray.

Using a food processor, cream together the softened butter and the caster sugar until it is fluffy and pale. Add the lightly beaten eggs, the flour and baking powder and mix well. Add the lemon zest and juice and mix again.

Pour the mix into the lined tin and level off gently. Pour the blueberries evenly on top. Bake for 30-35 minutes or until risen and a skewer inserted comes out clean.

While the sponge is still warm prick all over with a thin skewer or cocktail stick right down to the bottom. Mix together the lemon zest, juice and icing sugar, and pour over the sponge. Allow to cool before serving.

Orange, honey & almond syrup cake

A delicious and moist cake with a texture similar to a Rum Baba. It's extra special made with blood oranges as they have an exceptional flavour, so use them when they're in season (February/March in Italy).

Serve with full-fat Greek yoghurt.

Serves 12

100g fresh white breadcrumbs

450g caster sugar

225g ground almonds

300g sunflower oil

9 eggs

3 tsp baking powder

3 blood oranges, zest and juice separate

100g runny honey (if it's set honey, warm it before using)

Grease a 28cm-diameter silicone cake mould. Pre-heat the oven to 160°C (fan).

Mix together all the ingredients except the orange juice and the honey, either by hand or in a food processor. Pour into the cake mould and put the mould onto a baking sheet so it's easier to move around. Bake for 1-1¼ hours until the cake is light, golden brown and a sharp knife inserted comes out clean.

Mix the orange juice and honey together until blended.

When the cake has cooled, skewer holes all over it whilst it's still in the mould. Slowly and evenly pour the syrup over and let it soak in well. Leave for about 10 minutes, then ease it away from the edges with a palette knife and turn out onto a serving plate so that the top is on the bottom and vice versa. This means you have a lovely glisteningly moist top – as you can see in the picture opposite.

Carrot cake with cream cheese icing
& salted caramel walnut crumb

This is the moistest, gooiest carrot cake you can imagine. The quantities for the salted caramel walnut crumb make masses more than you need for this cake, but it's so delicious, you'll eat quite a lot as you're making it and the rest can be used on cakes, tossed into salads, added to the granola on page 41 or just nibbled as a snack.

Serves 8 generously using two 20cm loose-bottomed cake tins

2 eggs
200ml sunflower oil
1 tsp vanilla essence
100ml double cream
200g light muscovado sugar, any lumps broken up

200g wholemeal flour
½ tsp ground nutmeg
1 tsp cinnamon
1 tsp bicarbonate of soda
pinch of salt

225g carrots, peeled and grated
40g sultanas
40g walnuts, roughly chopped

375g full-fat cream cheese
60g salted butter
100g icing sugar
1 lemon, juice and zest

150g walnut pieces
75g caster sugar
25g butter
½ tsp salt

Grease and line two 20cm-diameter loose-bottomed cake tins.

Place the eggs, oil, vanilla, cream and sugar in a bowl and mix together by hand. In another large bowl stir together the flour, nutmeg, cinnamon, bicarbonate of soda and salt. Stir the wet mixture into the dry mixture and then, working quickly (do not leave the mixture to stand as the bicarbonate of soda will stop working after a time) stir in the grated carrot, sultanas and chopped walnuts. Divide between the two cake tins/moulds.

Bake at 140°C (fan) for 35 minutes. A sharp knife inserted should come out clean. Leave in the cake mould for 10 minutes and then ease out carefully to cool on a rack.

To make the icing, whizz the cream cheese, butter, sugar and lemon juice and zest in a food processor.

For the salted caramel walnut crunch, put all the remaining ingredients in a large frying pan. Warm over a medium heat, stirring regularly, until the sugar starts to melt (about 5 minutes). Stir constantly for a further 5 minutes until the nuts are totally coated in goo and beginning to smell toasted. Spread out immediately onto baking parchment and allow to cool.

Put into a food processor and pulse so that you have a mixture of roughly chopped and slightly powdered nuts/caramel.

Store in a little airtight plastic tub until needed.

To assemble the cake (only do this once the cakes have cooled completely), put the bottom layer on a large plate. Spread with about one third of the icing. Put the second layer on and spread with another third of the icing. Then spread the final lot of icing around the edge. Sprinkle the top generously with salted caramel walnut crumbs.

New York Times rhubarb torte

I was given this recipe by Sarah's wonderful late godmother, Helen Hyder. The cake is so named because the recipe (she told us) is reprinted year after year in the *New York Times* in response to constant reader requests. It's simple and adaptable. It works well with rhubarb, cherries, plums, raspberries, cranberries (best mixed with some pears), nectarines, peaches – anything with juice and some acidity.

Serves 8

1kg rhubarb, sliced 2cm

100g light muscovado sugar (for the rhubarb)

100g butter

100g light muscovado sugar

80g plain white flour

1 tsp baking powder

¼ tsp salt

2 eggs, beaten

½ lemon, juice of

1 dsp icing sugar

½ tsp ground cinnamon

Additional icing sugar for dusting

You'll need a 25cm loose-bottomed cake tin, greased and lined.

Pre-heat the oven to 150°C (fan). Toss the sliced rhubarb with 100g sugar, spread it out on a large baking sheet and cook for about 20 minutes until the rhubarb is just tender.

In a food processor, cream the butter and the other 100g sugar together. Add the flour, baking powder, salt and beaten eggs. Mix well.

Spoon the batter into the greased and lined tin, and arrange the cooked rhubarb on top.

If you're using different fruit, e.g. peaches, but not rhubarb, you may need to sprinkle it with a little lemon juice and sugar, depending on how sweet the fruit is.

Sprinkle a little cinnamon on top of the fruit.

Bake for 40-50 minutes or until the sponge is springy to touch.

Dust with icing sugar and serve either warm or at room temperature with a big dollop of crème fraîche.

Blackcurrant & plum streusel cake

This cake is good with most fruit but it's really superb with fruit at the more acidic end of the spectrum: damsons, plums, rhubarb, blackcurrant, cranberries, gooseberries and raspberries. Some fruit such as rhubarb, unripe plums and gooseberries will need pre-cooking, but not the softer fruit, such as blackcurrants and raspberries. Apples and pears will usually need pre-cooking.

It's very slightly adapted from *Seasonal Secrets*, the outpouring of several decades' cooking experience from Victoria O'Neill, Australian/Herefordian extraordinaire whose 'Cooking with Class' cookery school has delighted and engaged Herefordian cooks for many years and which is now winning friends in its new location in West London.

You can make this as a round cake for slicing but I prefer it as a tray bake.

For the middle

300g unripe plums chopped into 1cm pieces

75g light muscovado sugar (this will vary with the fruit – e.g. rhubarb needs more)

400g blackcurrants (fresh or frozen)

For the base

125g ground almonds

125g self-raising flour

75g light muscovado sugar

200g butter, diced

2 eggs, lightly beaten

For the streusel topping

175g light muscovado sugar (or whatever brown sugar you have)

125g plain flour

125g cold butter, diced

75g flaked almonds

1 tsp cinnamon

You'll need a 30cm x 40cm baking tray (at least 4cm deep).

Pre-heat the oven to 180°C (fan) and grease and line the baking tin.

Mix the chopped plums with the sugar, spread onto a baking tray and put in the pre-heated oven for about 10 minutes until they feel tender but not disintegrated. Take out of the oven and stir in the blackcurrants.

Prepare the base. Mix all the base ingredients except the eggs in a food mixer or food processor, until they look like breadcrumbs. Add the eggs and mix again to make a dough. Spread the dough into the base of the prepared cake tin and bake at 180°C (fan) for 15 minutes. It will have begun to firm up but won't look quite cooked.

Make the topping. Whizz the topping ingredients together – again either a food mixer or a food processor will do the job. If you want the flaked almonds to stay in large pieces then add them right at the end.

Spoon the fruit onto the partially cooked base. Spoon the topping evenly on top of the fruit. Cook at 180°C (fan) for about 35 minutes, until the topping is beginning to brown.

Try to leave it to cool a little before devouring. It's good both warm and at room temperature.

The best mince pies

We don't start Christmassy stuff at the cafés too early but as soon as we start making these they are scoffed at a challengingly speedy rate.

I love mince pies but I only love really good mince pies. What I want is a high proportion of mincemeat to pastry; excellent well-balanced and fruity mincemeat; and a good crumbly pastry. These mince pies are the business. The recipe includes a bit from Gary Rhodes, a bit from Delia and a bit from me. I think it's well worth making your own mincemeat – actually it's very straightforward and gives you the chance to customize the recipe to suit your taste.

The pastry makes about 12 pies depending on the size of your pie tins/moulds.

Makes about 2.5kg of mincemeat (enough for 100 mince pies)

Mincemeat

500g Bramley apples, cored and diced very small (pea-sized), no need to peel

250g pre-shredded vegetarian suet

500g raisins

375g sultanas

250g mixed candied peel, diced

350g light muscovado sugar

2 lemons, juice and zest

2 oranges, juice and zest

2 dsp mixed spice

½ tsp ground cinnamon

¼ tsp nutmeg

100ml ginger wine

For making the mince pies

Mince pie pastry – see page 251

1 egg, lightly beaten with a pinch of salt for glazing

To make the mincemeat

Put everything apart from the ginger wine into a large mixing bowl and mix thoroughly. Cover the bowl with some foil and put in the oven at 120°C (fan) for about 2 hours until the apple is tender. Take out of the oven and stir in the ginger wine. Store in pre-warmed sterilized jam jars or in Tupperware in the fridge.

To make the mince pies

You can make the mince pies any size you like; I use pie moulds which are 7cm diameter and 2.5cm deep with flat bottoms (you don't get enough filling in the sloping-sided ones). The pastry will come about threequarters of the way up the sides of the mould, so any overspill of mincemeat juice won't go all over the place.

Roll out the pastry quite thin and cut out circles using a 9cm-diameter cutter (keep some pastry aside to make small stars for the tops). Place the pastry neatly in the pie mould, pushing it well into the corners and making the top rim reasonably even.

Put 35g mincemeat (one good dsp) into each one and then top with a star of pastry. Brush with a little beaten egg and bake for about 15 minutes at 180°C (fan oven) until golden and crisp. Leave to cool for 10 mins in the tin and then transfer to a cooling rack. Dust generously with icing sugar to serve.

These mince pies stay good for days, but they are at their very best when still just a little warm from the oven.

Food for feasting

This chapter is all about relaxed celebration – cooking for larger numbers of people in a non-stressy way.

It's easy to get worried about cooking for a crowd, but the whole process of cooking – even for a big feast – can be and should be a pleasure, not a punishment. Don't be too ambitious, nobody needs food that's desperately trying to reach the Masterchef final. Pizza, pulled pork in a bun, brisket in red wine with creamy mash: these are dishes that will win friends and influence people.

Try to think through the whole cooking and serving process and plan what can be done in advance. If you've got a house full of people, work out which things can be delegated – this might include last-minute shopping for crucial things you've forgotten. I find that people enjoy joining in as long as they're given clear instructions and there's a glass of wine to assist the process.

For the overnight-cooked meat recipes (slow lamb with chilli and ketchup, DIY hog roast, pulled pork and pulled brisket) it's worth mentioning the fan/non-fan oven issue. The quantities of liquid given and the temperatures are all for fan ovens, in order to be consistent with the rest of the book. However, non-fan ovens – and especially Aga-type ovens – are particularly good for this sort of cooking as they allow more moisture retention. So if you have a non-fan alternative, this is the moment to use it, and you can probably cut the amount of water in the recipe somewhat. How much will depend on each individual oven – if in doubt use the quantity in the recipe. Don't forget to add 20°C to all temperatures if you're using a non-fan oven.

To 'pull' slow-cooked meat, use two large forks and pull in opposite directions along the grain of the meat.

Most of the recipes in the '5 wholesome hotpots' chapter and the 'Lunches from the café oven' chapter work well cooked in big quantities too. For the pizza recipe given here, I list a choice of toppings, because pizza is the ultimate crowd-pleaser – small children, teenagers and most adults seem to be pretty happy about the idea of getting proper home-made pizza at a party. All that's needed is good dough, a straightforward and tasty tomato sauce and toppings to suit!

Holiday pasta bake with fennel sausage & roast veg

Most summers we go on holiday with the cousins – up to twenty of us in a house in France or Italy. It's blissful. We've been doing it since all the (seven) kids were tiny but now they'll sometimes cook for us, and in recent years this has been their dish of choice. It's rich, comforting and deeply satisfying, particularly if you can get hold of real Italian-type fennel sausages. You could easily make this dish veggie by taking out the mozzarella and sausages and substituting 300g cooked puy lentils (cooked weight) and 450g crumbled feta – both added at the point where the dish is assembled before baking. Serve with a simple green salad.

Serves 10

2 medium aubergines, diced 2cm
3 tbs olive oil (for the aubergines)
½ tsp salt

2 red peppers, sliced thickly
2 yellow peppers, sliced thickly
2 tbs olive oil (for the peppers)
½ tsp salt

1 large onion (about 300g), chopped
2 tbs olive oil (for the onion)
½ tsp salt
2 cloves garlic, crushed
1 tsp dried oregano
8 fennel sausages or other good sausages (550g), in 2cm chunks
1500g passata (3 packets)

600g pasta (penne is good)

3 x 150g blobs mozzarella, roughly torn
200g good cheddar, grated
100g Parmesan, grated

Pre-heat the oven to 180°C (fan). Toss the vegetables, separately, in their olive oil and salt. Roast the aubergines for 30 minutes and the peppers for 25 minutes until both are browning at the edges and quite soft.

In a large wide pan sweat the onion in the olive oil and salt. After a couple of minutes add the crushed garlic and oregano and continue to cook on a medium heat for about 10 minutes until the onion is soft. Add the chopped sausages and continue to cook for a further 10 minutes, stirring from time to time. Add the passata and bring to the boil. Turn down the heat very low, put a lid on and simmer for a further 30 minutes.

Bring a large pan of water to the boil and salt generously. Put in the pasta and cook for 2 minutes less than the instructions on the packet say (the pasta will cook for a bit longer in the oven). Drain.

In a large bowl, mix the nearly-cooked pasta with the sausage/tomato sauce and the roast peppers and aubergines.

In a very large baking/lasagne dish (say 40 x 30 x 7cm) or two smaller ones, put half the pasta mixture. Then scatter the mozzarella evenly on top. Put the rest of the pasta mix on top and finish with the mixed grated Parmesan and cheddar.

Bake at 160°C (fan) for 25-30 minutes until brown on top and hot all the way through (this assumes you cook it straight away and the constituent parts are still warm. If you allow it to cool completely before final cooking it will take longer to heat through).

Pizza for parties

For the many kids' pizza parties we've had at home over the last twenty years we've often got the children rolling their own dough and doing their own toppings. I like the combination of mozzarella (particularly buffalo mozzarella) and cheddar, although it's clearly not authentic. Marinated and roast tofu may not be to everyone's taste but made a vegan pizza-eater very happy on the evening this photo was taken. The cooking method – baking in a very hot oven but without a pizza stone – is also non-authentic but it's simple and it works. I give a recipe for a nice tomato sauce on page 241, but if you're in a rush you can make an acceptable pizza using passata straight from the jar or packet. Bear in mind that unless you have remarkably capacious ovens, the pizzas won't all appear at the same time – but then, people do like sharing and chatting and are usually happy to have some as and when it's ready.

Makes 8 medium-sized individual pizzas (about 150g dough for each base)

1 batch of dough (see page 23, or page 25 if you start the day before)

For the tomato sauce

see page 241

For the toppings

4 x 125g blobs mozzarella

250g strong cheddar, grated

Then choose from:

roast peppers

goats' cheese (omit the other cheeses)

anchovies

spicy sausage

olives and capers

cooked ham (and pineapple!)

prosciutto

chopped-up marinated and roast tofu

Make the dough at least a couple of hours or more in advance – just keep knocking it back if you're not ready to use it.

About an hour and a half before you want to eat, roll out the pizzas. They can be any shape and about 3mm thick. I like long oval/rectangular pizzas currently. One of the nice things about home-made pizzas is having them come out different and irregular shapes. I reckon that 100g dough makes a child-sized pizza, 150g an adult-sized pizza and 200g dough a hungry-teenager pizza. Put the pizza bases on lightly-floured baking sheets as you roll them out, and leave to prove for at least 40 minutes – they can happily survive an hour or two more than that if it suits your timing.

Put a modest ladleful of tomato sauce on each pizza, spreading it thinly and getting close to the edge but leaving roughly 1cm of dough un-sauced. Add your toppings, finishing with any cheeses that you're using.

Bake at 220°C for 12-14 minutes until the cheese is bubbling and the base is cooked.

DIY hog roast

In our local village we have an annual Hog Rog. This is a Rogation walk (traditional beating of the parish bounds) followed by a hog roast. The first year we did this, the hog roast was a little disappointing, and too expensive to raise any funds for our fund-raiser. So now neighbours Rob and Ed and I each make a slow-cooked pork shoulder – there's a modest competitive spirit between us which results in very good pork all round – a DIY hog roast.

Slow-roast pork shoulder has become a modern classic. This version is simpler than most and stunningly delicious. Spianata (page 31) or ciabatta rolls (page 25) are the ideal eating vehicles for this, particularly when accompanied by apple sauce (page 225) and summer salads.

As with other very slow-cooked meat dishes you can either cook it overnight or during the day, depending on when you want to eat. If you're serving this to a large number of people who are queuing up for their porky bun, you ideally want some means of keeping the meat/cooking juices warm, close to where you're serving.

Serves around 15

4kg shoulder of pork on the bone, with the skin scored

6 good cloves garlic, peeled

4 tbs fennel seeds

2 dsp salt

500ml cider

500ml water

Pre-heat the oven to 200°C (fan). Using a pestle and mortar or small food processor make a rough paste of the garlic, fennel seeds and salt. Put the pork in a roasting tin and rub half the paste into the skin side of the pork, working it into the slits in the skin where possible. Then turn it over and do the same to the flesh side.

Put the pork into the hot oven for half an hour, skin side up. Add the cider and water, cover the tray tightly with baking foil, put it back for 10 minutes for the cider and water to heat up, and then turn down to 120°C (fan). Roast for 8-12 hours or overnight.

About half an hour before you want to eat, take the pork out of the oven, turn the oven back up to 220°C (fan) and slice the skin off the pork, discarding any excess fat clinging to it. Slice or cut the crackling into thin strips and put it on a clean roasting tray. Return to the now-hot oven for 10-20 minutes to create lovely crunchy crackling. Watch the crackling carefully so it doesn't burn.

Meanwhile slice the meat into thick chunks, returning them to the cidery juices as you cut. As soon as the crackling is done you're ready to eat and create much happiness for many people. Make sure everyone gets their fair share of the cooking juices as well as the meat itself.

A simple gammon feast

This is a great simple celebratory meal. Gammon is a forgiving piece of meat – its flavour is beautiful just as it is and it's the perfect foil for the rich variety and lovely colours of the vegetable accompaniments this feast offers. Just boil the joint for roughly the right amount of time and don't throw away the liquid you've boiled it in – it'll be perfect for soups and risottos in the days to come (see pages 63 and 145).

Gammons are cut in various different ways – the larger cuts give you the best slices of meat. When thinking about leftovers, just compare the price of this delicious ham with what you can buy at a supermarket. If your leftovers are too overwhelming, then freeze chunks of the ham for later deliciousness.

Don't forget that if you're cooking a very big gammon you will need a very large pan with a lid. Older cookbooks talk about pre-soaking before cooking to get rid of excess saltiness, but this is not now generally necessary. Serve with butternut squash purée (page 237), roast beetroots with balsamic vinegar and crème fraîche (page 237), and spring greens with butter and mustard (page 236).

Calculate the simmering time as 50 minutes per kg plus 25 minutes.

Serves 20 – or fewer to allow for plenty of leftovers

5kg smoked gammon

1kg carrots, peeled and cut into large chunks

4kg waxy potatoes such as Ratte, Charlotte or Pink Fir Apple

3 tbs olive oil

2 tsp salt

freshly ground black pepper

For the apple sauce

1kg bramley apples, peeled, cored and roughly chopped

100g sugar

Put the gammon in a large pan with enough cold water to just cover the meat. Bring to the boil and simmer gently for the necessary time (see above). Add the carrots about an hour before the meat is due to be ready. If you're not going to eat at that moment, leave the gammon in the pan with the cooking water (with the heat turned off) until you are ready. If you're uncertain whether your gammon is cooked, look for an internal temperature at the thickest part of the joint of at least 72°C. Keep the cooking water for ham stock, for soup or risotto (see pages 63 and 145).

While the gammon is cooking, prepare the rest of the accompaniments. Boil the potatoes for 20-25 minutes until they are just tender. Drain, cut in half and toss them back in the pan, with the olive oil, salt and pepper and leave with the lid on in a warm place until you're ready to eat. If you've got a good place to keep them warm they'll keep very happily for an hour or more.

Put the apples and sugar in a lidded pan. Put on a low heat with the lid on. Cook for about 10 minutes until the apple is completely mushy – at least that's how I like it. Keep the apple sauce warm until you need it.

Pulled beef brisket

This is an astonishingly tasty Herefordshire version (hence the cider) of a southern USA classic. For a relaxed party, it's great to serve with either brioche buns (see page 37) or spianata (as pictured here – see page 31), and with a good coleslaw (see page 133) and a cold beer (see the fridge!).

I think it makes sense to make quite a big quantity of this and then freeze what you don't want straight away. Or try it the next day with crumpets, roast tomatoes and melted cheese (see page 255). Or you could add some passata to some of it – together with some cheese sauce, it makes a very delicious lasagne.

If you're not used to cooking things overnight, then have courage and give it a go – it's bizarre but rather wonderful to wake up to the aroma of slowly cooking spiced beef.

Serves 15-20 depending on your appetite

2 tsp fennel seeds, toasted and whizzed in a spice grinder or ground with a pestle and mortar

2 tsp fresh rosemary, finely chopped

2 cloves garlic, crushed

20g salt

2 tsp hot smoked paprika

2kg beef brisket boned but not rolled (if you can only get a rolled one then just cut the string and unroll it so that it's easier to rub the spices into it)

500ml dry cider

75g molasses or black treacle

Pre-heat the oven to 200°C (fan).

Mix together the ground fennel seeds, rosemary, garlic, salt and hot smoked paprika. Rub the spice mix over all the meat's surfaces and try to get it into any nooks and crannies. Put into a heavy casserole dish with a well-fitting lid.

Roast for 30 minutes with the lid off. Mix the cider and molasses together and pour over the meat. Put the lid on, turn the oven down to 120°C (fan) and cook overnight (or for 10-12 hours) until a lot of fat has run out and the meat is soft enough to be pulled with a fork.

Pour off all the liquid (including any melted fat); put in a gravy separator and discard the fat. Discard any remaining solid fat and any gristly bits (there shouldn't be much of this) and pull the beef with a couple of forks. Put the pulled meat and the liquid together and mix well. You can either serve it straight away or keep in the fridge and fry it up in a pan, or warm it in the oven when you want it. It's resilient stuff.

Brisket of beef with red wine & mushrooms

As well as our regular daytime café business, we open in the evenings at both my cafés for weddings, birthday parties and similar events. This delicious brisket dish is by far the most popular choice of main course at these parties. If you're not familiar with slow-cooked brisket it's well worth discovering. Much better value than prime roasting joints, it has for me the most beefy flavour of all and is wonderfully tender if properly cooked.

The brisket is poached long and slow in red wine. Then you make an onion, mushroom and red wine sauce flavoured with the cooking liquor from the beef. Finally the brisket is thickly sliced and served with a generous ladleful of the sauce. Delicious with parsnip and potato mash and slow-cooked red cabbage and apple.

Some chefs say that it matters hugely what sort of wine you use in cooking. It may be that my palate is insufficiently good, but to my taste a fairly plonky red works beautifully here. You can do the main cooking the day before, and then on the day of the feast gently re-heat the thickly sliced meat in its sauce.

Serves 10

2kg boned and rolled brisket

1 bottle red wine

4 good sprigs of thyme

1 tbs soy sauce

1 tsp salt

500ml water

500g onion, diced 1cm

½ a bulb of garlic, crushed

1 tsp salt

100g butter

50ml olive oil

500g mushrooms – closed or open cap are both fine

35g flour

Put the brisket in a wide heavy-bottomed pan with a lid. The meat should fill most of the dish so that the liquid comes about half way up the joint. Add the wine, thyme, soy sauce, salt and water. Bring to the boil and then turn down very low so that the liquid is only just simmering. Put the lid on and simmer gently for 4 hours. About halfway through the cooking time, turn the brisket over so that the other half is submerged in the cooking liquor. Once the brisket is cooked, take it out of its poaching liquid and put on one side for slicing. Keep the poaching liquid warm.

In a separate pan sweat the onion and garlic with the salt in the butter and olive oil until soft. Add the mushrooms and cook until soft. Then add the flour to the onion/mushroom mix and continue cooking for a couple of minutes whilst stirring. Gradually add the poaching liquid to the onion/mushroom flour mix, stirring thoroughly with each addition. When all the liquid has been added keep cooking and stirring for a couple more minutes. Adjust the consistency with more water if necessary. Check the seasoning and adjust as necessary with salt and freshly ground black pepper.

Finally slice the brisket fairly thickly, add back to the sauce and put on a low heat. Make sure the brisket is thoroughly hot before serving.

Pulled pork

Pulled pork isn't pretty but goodness it's delicious– proper caveman food. It was ultra-fashionable a few years ago – though pulled pork on pizza was (for me) a step too far. But pulled pork in a brioche bun with roast pepper ketchup and coleslaw – now you're talking.

Our spice rub is very minimally adapted from one used by the renowned Pitt Cue company, specialists in barbecued food from the Deep South. Serve with roast pepper ketchup (page 241) and coleslaw (page 133) in either a ciabatta (page 25) or brioche bun (page 37), with salad leaves on the side. A lot of places serve pulled pork with a gloopy barbecue sauce, but I prefer this method of mixing the meat with the juices/sauce.

Start the day before you plan to eat.

Serves 15-20

Spice rub

5g fennel seeds

½ tsp cumin

½ tsp black peppercorns

½ tsp coriander seeds

75g light muscovado sugar

5g garlic powder

50g salt

10g sweet smoked paprika

15g paprika

½ tsp dried oregano

½ tsp cayenne

4kg pork shoulder, boned and skinned but not rolled

Sauce ingredients

1 litre water

120g molasses

120g Dijon mustard

It's worth putting in all the spice-rub ingredients, even though the list is annoyingly long! Toast the fennel, cumin, black peppercorns and coriander, then grind to a fine powder. Add all the rest of the spice-rub ingredients and mix together well. Rub onto the raw meat, working it into all the cracks and crannies.

Pre-heat the oven to 200°C (fan). Roast the meat for 30 minutes. Mix the sauce ingredients together. Take the meat out of the oven and pour the sauce mixture into the bottom of the tray. Cover the tray with foil, sealing as well as possible around the edges.

Turn the oven down to 120°C (fan) and cook overnight (or for about 12 hours, but the timing is not critical) until the meat is so soft that you can pull it off with a fork.

Pull the pork – use two forks like for roast duck in Chinese restaurants. I learned from Pitt Cue an excellent piece of pulled pork jargon: they stress the importance of developing a good 'bark', i.e. the browned edge of the meat that develops during the slow-roasting. So when you pull the meat you've got mostly soft pinkish/brownish interior with flecks of tasty spicy well-browned exterior meat. Yum.

Mix the pulled meat with the sauce and any juices/fat which have come out of the pork during the overnight roast.

Once the meat and juices are mixed they re-heat very well.

Bill's Kitchen
Hereford

Slow lamb with chilli paste
& roast pepper ketchup

This is a variation on and simplification of Hugh Fearnley-Whittingstall's Merguez lamb, introduced to us by our lamb-loving partly Patagonian sheep-farming cousins. It's spicy, delicious and incredibly straightforward if you've got some chilli paste and roast pepper ketchup already on the go. Decent shop-bought harissa and Heinz Ketchup also works, but look for good-quality harissa if you're going down this route, as it can be insufficiently punchy.

Serve with rice or couscous and perhaps some kale stir-fried with whole cumin seeds and finished with a squeeze of lemon. It's also wonderful with baba ganoush (page 119) in a bun.

Like the other slow-cooked dishes, this is cooked long and slow in the oven, either overnight (if you want it for lunchtime) or during the day (if you want to eat it in the evening). This also re-heats very well.

Serves 6-8 depending on your appetite

2 tsp chilli paste (page 247)

200g roast pepper ketchup (page 241)

2 tsp salt

1.7kg lamb shoulder on the bone

500ml water

Mix chilli paste, ketchup and salt. Make cuts in the lamb and work the marinade in. Leave in the fridge for 2-4 hours, then put in a heavy lidded casserole dish with the water. Pre-heat the oven to 120°C (fan). Bring to the boil on the hob and then put the lid on and cook in the oven overnight (11-13 hours).

Take the lamb out of the oven, pour the juices into a gravy separator, discard the fat, and retain the spicy juices. Slice the lamb thickly, discarding the bones and any pure bits of fat. Serve with the spicy juices in a gravy jug to pour over.

Bits & pieces: relishes, sauces, dressings & pastries

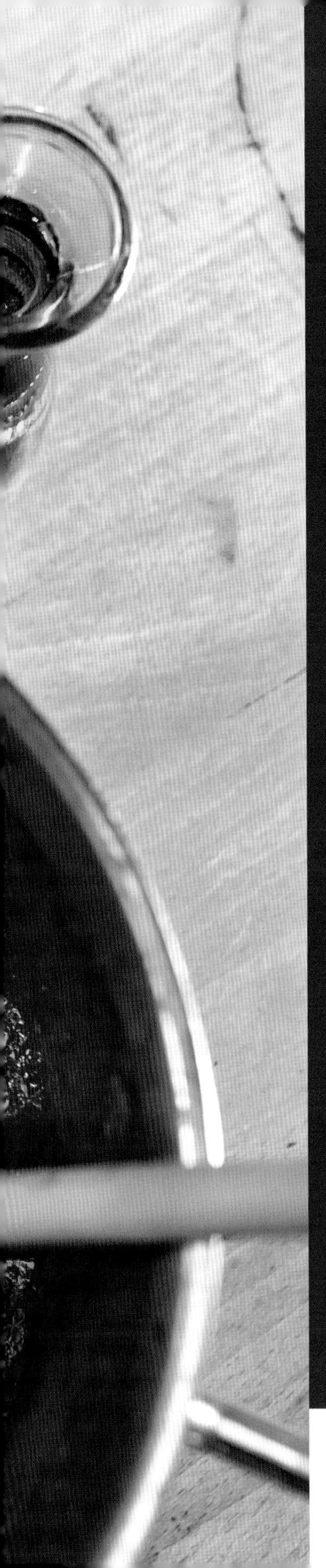

This chapter does what it says on the tin. There's lots of crucial recipes in here – pastries, side-dishes, sauces, dressings – which don't constitute dishes in their own right, but are necessary either to create other dishes or to accompany them. And below, I give my favourite recipe for cooking green veg. Out of all the recipes in the book this is probably the one that I use at home most frequently.

The best and simplest method for green vegetables

Lots of people have told me that they've found this very basic method revelatory. It's for serving the vegetable as a simple accompaniment – there are of course many delicious and more elaborate ways of incorporating green vegetables into more complex dishes.

There is a theory that you should steam all green vegetables but I don't personally find it a reliable method. Probably my two favourite and most consistently enjoyed green vegetables at home are sweetheart cabbage and our own runner beans. For both (and for broccoli, broad beans and asparagus) I follow the simplest possible method that I think produces utterly reliably excellent results.

Slice the vegetables finely, particularly the runner beans (if you cut them in too-thick pieces, then the outside of each piece will be cooked before the inside, so you would need to cook them for longer to achieve overall tenderness, and then the outside of each piece would be slightly overcooked).

Use a large pan of boiling water. It's like cooking pasta: you want quite a lot of water relative to the quantity of veg so that it cooks quickly and evenly. Don't add salt as you will season after cooking.

Add the thinly cut cabbage or beans to the boiling water. Bring back to the boil and keep boiling fairly vigorously. For cabbage boil for one minute, for runner beans 2-3 minutes (for broccoli just 30 seconds).

Drain very thoroughly and toss in a little olive oil and salt. Of course if you don't like salt then don't add it, but for me this combination provides maximum pleasure.

Serve straight away – this is not a job to do in advance.

Spring greens with butter & mustard

This is so simple it's barely a recipe. It's a delicious accompaniment to rich meat dishes like the beef and ale pie on page 89. Try using cavolo nero as an alternative to spring greens.

This amount of mustard gives a strong mustardy flavour – feel free to reduce it if you're looking for a gentler taste.

Serves 6

500g spring greens finely shredded (cut out any fat stalks)

50g butter

3 tsp Dijon mustard

Bring a large pan of water to the boil. Add the spring greens and simmer for a couple of minutes until barely tender. Drain thoroughly. Put the butter and mustard in the pan. Melt the butter and mix thoroughly with the mustard. Add back the cooked greens and stir thoroughly. Serve.

Butternut squash, thyme & lemon purée

This is a velvety smooth and aromatic accompaniment for anything with gravy. It's very good with gammon (page 225) , coq au vin, beef and ale pie (page 89) or a red wine and mushroom ragout, alongside Dauphinoise potatoes (page 239) and some Savoy cabbage.

1 medium/large (800g to 1200g) butternut squash

1 dsp fresh thyme leaves, stripped from the stalks

1 lemon – all of zest, half of juice

50g butter, melted

salt and freshly ground black pepper

Pre-heat the oven to 180°C (fan). Wrap the squash in foil and bake for about 2-3 hours until very soft. Allow to cool sufficiently to handle. Peel and de-seed. Purée the squash in a food processor with the rest of the ingredients.

To serve this just re-warm slowly on the hob, stirring regularly, or heat in a covered dish in a medium oven.

Roast beetroot with balsamic vinegar & crème fraîche

This is fantastic with gammon (page 225) and other piggy feasts. It works well both hot and cold.

Full-fat plain yoghurt is a fine alternative to the crème fraîche.

Serves 6

500g raw beetroot, preferably not too big

1 tbs sunflower oil

2 tsp balsamic vinegar

50g crème fraîche

Pre-heat the oven to 180°C (fan). Put the beetroots in a roasting tin and turn them in the sunflower oil. Cover with foil and roast for about 1½ hours until the beetroots feel tender when pierced with a sharp knife.

Allow to cool and then peel. Cut them into 3cm chunks and then toss in the balsamic vinegar and crème fraîche. To serve hot re-heat gently in a heavy-bottomed lidded pan.

Rosemary roast potatoes

If you are a customer at either of my cafés you will be very familiar with the sight of these lovely potatoes. They're the nearest we come to chips (not very near) and they seem to go remarkably well with a wide variety of dishes. They are also extremely simple to prepare.

Serves 6

1.2kg small potatoes (e.g. Charlottes), halved

3 tbs olive oil

1 tsp salt

¼ tsp freshly ground black pepper

2 sprigs fresh rosemary, leaves stripped from stalks and finely chopped

Pre-heat the oven to 180°C (fan). Mix everything very well together and spread out on large baking tray. Bake for 35-45 minutes until the potatoes are browning and completely tender.

Rosemary roast potatoes

Dauphinoise potatoes

Patatas bravas with chilli paste

Dauphinoise potatoes

This is a rich and delicious accompaniment, very good with wine- or cider-based dishes such as the brisket with red wine and mushrooms on page 229 or the belly pork on page 159. It's easy to prepare in advance, and once ready it can sit in an oven at low heat for half an hour or more until you're ready for it.

300ml double cream

125ml milk

1 clove garlic, crushed

1 tsp salt

freshly ground black pepper

a scrape of freshly ground nutmeg (optional)

1kg potatoes (e.g. Maris Piper) sliced ½ cm, peeled or unpeeled

Put the cream and milk into a large pan along with the garlic and salt and pepper and nutmeg if you're using it, and bring to the boil over a medium-low heat. Turn off the heat.

Add the sliced potatoes to a large pan of boiling water. Bring back to the boil and then simmer for 3-5 minutes until the potatoes are just losing their hardness but are not quite cooked. Drain.

Pre-heat the oven to 150°C (fan). Grease an ovenproof dish (30cm x 20cm x 5cm) with butter. Pour the potatoes into the dish and spread them out evenly. Pour the cream mixture on top, being sure that all the top layer of potatoes get some cream on them as you are pouring. Bake for 50 minutes to an hour until lightly browned and the potatoes are tender.

Patatas bravas with chilli paste

This is the omnipresent item on tapas menus – potatoes with a spicy tomato sauce. As well as being a snack in their own right they go beautifully with our courgette and feta filo pie (page 85) or Spanakopita.

If you don't have chilli paste to hand you can just use chilli flakes or harissa paste for a slightly different flavour. If you like your patatas particularly brave you can increase the amount of chilli paste.

750g small potatoes, halved (Charlottes are ideal)

4 tbs olive oil

1 tsp salt

1 large onion, halved and sliced

4 tbs olive oil

1 tsp salt

1 x 500g packet passata

2 tsp chilli paste (see page 247)

Pre-heat the oven to 180°C (fan). Toss the halved potatoes with the oil and salt and roast for around 35 minutes until browning and quite tender.

Meanwhile fry the onion on a lowish heat in the olive oil with the salt for about 25 minutes until very soft. Add the passata and chilli paste, bring to the boil and simmer for about 15 minutes to reduce and thicken the sauce.

Mix the sauce with the roast potatoes and serve straight away.

Leeky mash

A slight variation on colcannon, that's particularly good with lamb dishes – it's pictured with the lamb with puy lentils and lemon on page 170.

Serves 6

500g leeks, halved, sliced 1cm, washed and drained

2 tbs olive oil

½ tsp salt

1kg potatoes, peeled and diced 2cm

100ml milk

100g butter

a little freshly grated nutmeg

1 tsp salt

¼ tsp freshly ground black pepper

Sweat the leeks in the olive oil and salt on a low heat in a covered pan for 7-10 minutes until just tender but not mushy, and put aside.

In a large pan cook the peeled and chopped potatoes until the potatoes are really soft but not over-cooked and breaking up. Drain the potatoes and then heat the milk and butter together in the same pan until the butter is melted.

Put the cooked potatoes through a potato ricer (or failing that, mash with a potato masher). Beat vigorously with the butter/milk mixture and the nutmeg, salt and pepper and then stir in the leeks.

Courgettes with tomato & basil

We eat a lot of this at home when our courgette plants are in full flood. It's delicious as a light lunch with a bit of feta crumbled on top and some good bread, as a simple sauce for pasta or as an accompaniment to a dish like the Parmesan, leek and lentil bake on page 103.

Serves 4

2 tbs olive oil

600g courgettes, halved and sliced on the bias 1cm

2 cloves garlic, crushed

1 tsp salt

300g fresh plum tomatoes (or other good cooking tomatoes), diced 1cm

15g basil, roughly torn or chopped

freshly ground black pepper

Heat the oil in a very large frying pan. On high heat, add the courgettes, spread out only one layer deep. Stir only every 2-3 minutes so the courgettes have a chance to brown.

After the first stir, add the garlic and salt. After about 8 minutes the courgettes should be beginning to colour a bit on each side. Stir in the tomatoes for about 30 seconds, then take off the heat and stir in the basil and black pepper.

Note: this method produces fairly firm courgettes. However, I've recently been introduced by both my niece Grace and our friend Tom Graham to courgettes cooked longer (maybe 30 minutes or more) and slower which gives a quite different but also very delicious texture. Take your choice!

Roast pepper ketchup

This has enough chilli to provide gentle warmth – add more if you like it hot. It will keep happily in the fridge for a week, and is also good with cheese on toast, as a pasta sauce or as an accompaniment to cold meat.

Makes just over 1 litre of ketchup

2 tbs olive oil

900g red peppers (5 or 6), cut into fat strips

1 medium onion, roughly chopped

1 tsp salt

2 cloves garlic, crushed

1 tsp dried chilli flakes (jalapeno are good)

1 x 500g packet passata

1 tsp white wine vinegar

½ tsp sugar

Pre-heat the oven to 180°C (fan). Toss the peppers in half the olive oil, spread out on a roasting tray and roast for about 25 minutes until they are beginning to brown and are very tender.

Sweat the onion in the rest of the olive oil with the salt for about twenty minutes until very soft and sweet. Add the crushed garlic and chilli flakes and cook for a couple more minutes. Then add the passata, vinegar and sugar and simmer for a further twenty minutes.

Take off the heat, add the roast peppers and blend very thoroughly. Check the seasoning.

Best served at room temperature rather than fridge cold.

Tomato sauce for pizza

This is a useful, simple and tasty tomato sauce, adaptable to many different dishes.

Makes enough for the pizza on page 221

1 small onion, diced 2cm

1 clove garlic

½ tsp dried oregano

1 tsp salt

2 tbs olive oil

2 x 500g packets passata

Sweat the onion, garlic, salt and oregano in the olive oil for about 15 minutes until the onion is soft. Add the passata, bring to the boil and simmer for about 15 minutes on a lowish heat so that it thickens a little. Blitz with a handheld blender and check the seasoning.

Ian's spiced chickpeas

Ian's spiced chickpeas

Whilst I was (for ten years) a vegetarian, my mother was always concerned about my protein intake. I've inherited this concern and I'm always keen to make sure that there is enough protein in vegetarian dishes. So whilst ratatouille and tabouleh make a really tasty lunch, the nutritionist (and Jewish mother manqué) in me thinks it's even better when accompanied by these chickpeas or perhaps by some chilli-roast tofu. They're also delicious to eat on their own or as part of a meze.

This recipe originally came from the lovely Ian Burleigh when he was the manager at my erstwhile London café, The Place Below.

Serves 6 as an accompaniment

2 tbs coriander seeds

1 tbs cumin seeds

2 x 400g tins of chickpeas, drained (after you've drained them this will be about 450g chickpeas)

3 tbs olive oil

1 tsp salt

1 tsp hot smoked paprika

Toast the cumin and coriander seeds either in the oven or in a dry frying pan until they are just beginning to smell toasted. Allow to cool and then grind in a spice grinder.

Mix with the drained chickpeas, the olive oil, salt and freshly ground spices and hot smoked paprika and re-heat over a medium heat.

Herby bulghur

This is a kind of simplified warm tabouleh. It's good with roast aubergine ratatouille (page 109) and perfect with Lownz's lamb tagine (as in the picture on page 166).

Serves 6

250g coarse bulghur wheat

650ml boiling water

1 tsp salt

1 tbs olive oil

30g mint, roughly chopped

30g flat leaf parsley, roughly chopped

1 lemon, juice of

Put the bulghur wheat and the measured amount of boiling water and salt in a lidded pan. Bring to the boil and simmer on a very low heat with the lid on for 5-8 minutes until all the water has been absorbed (if you are using fine bulghur wheat or couscous, which are both acceptable alternatives, then just soak in the boiling water rather than simmering).

Stir in the rest of the ingredients and serve.

Roast garlic mayo

Roast garlic mayo

I'm not generally a massive fan of mayonnaise with everything, but there are a few things where it's essential – such as cold or poached chicken or the chorizo burgers on page 165.

The roast garlic on its own gives a nutty mellow taste which I like. If you like it more aggressively garlicky then add half a clove of raw crushed garlic.

Makes a good jam jar-full of mayo

3 good-sized cloves garlic, separated but not peeled

1 tbs white wine vinegar

2 egg yolks

½ tsp English mustard

300ml sunflower

50ml tepid water

Pre-heat the oven to 160°C (fan). Put the separated but not peeled garlic cloves on a baking sheet in the oven for about 15 minutes until just beginning to feel squidgy rather than firm. Allow to cool and then peel.

Put everything except the sunflower oil and water into a blender and whizz until smooth. Keep whizzing whilst slowly adding the sunflower oil. If it becomes too thick to whizz properly then add some water to thin it down a little, then continue with the oil. Add a bit more water as necessary until you have the desired mayo consistency. Season to taste with salt and pepper.

Cep sauce

This sauce can happily be made a day or two in advance.

25g dried ceps

200ml hot water (for soaking the ceps)

1 dsp sunflower oil

1 small onion, finely diced

1 clove garlic, crushed

¼ small chilli, finely chopped, without the seeds

¼ tsp salt

100g field mushrooms, finely diced

125ml red wine

2 tsp soy sauce

½ tsp sugar

1 tsp arrowroot (a gluten-free thickener)

cold water to mix

Soak the ceps in the hot water for about 30 minutes.

In a saucepan, sweat the onion, garlic, chilli and salt in the oil until soft. Add the diced field mushrooms and cook until soft, then add the wine, soy sauce and sugar. With a slotted spoon, take the ceps from their liquid and add them. Strain the liquid from the ceps through a fine sieve and add this too. Bring to the boil and simmer for about five minutes with the lid off, allowing the sauce to reduce a little.

Mix the arrowroot with a few drops of cold water and add half of it to the sauce. Bring back to the boil, stirring well. If you would like the sauce to be thicker, repeat the process with the rest of the arrowroot mixture, otherwise leave it as it is. Check the seasoning.

Chicken stock

If you have a roast chicken carcass left over (see the recipe for roast chicken, page 151), you can make a delicious and very simple chicken stock, perfect for soups and risottos like the ones on pages 63 and 147.

Bones from roast chicken carcass

cold water to cover

Put all the bones in a pan, broken up a bit so that they pack in nicely. Cover with water, bring to the boil and simmer for a couple of hours – or even better overnight in an Aga if you have one. Then strain off the liquid. You should end up with a good litre of excellent chicken stock.

If your chicken came with giblets then add them along with the bones.

Raita

Raita

A fragrant and cooling accompaniment to all things spicy – particularly good with the chilli and lemon roast chicken on page 76.

Serves 6 very generously

500g plain yoghurt

1 cucumber, grated and strained

30g mint, leaves stripped from the stalks and finely chopped

½ clove garlic, crushed

½ tsp salt

Mix everything together – nothing else to it!

Ras el hanout

This is a classic spice mix from Morocco, where apparently it means 'top of the shop', no doubt alluding to the high quality and possibly high prices of the spices used.

This recipe will make enough for several tagines – you should try it with Lownz's lamb tagine (see page 167).

1 cinnamon stick

1 tsp cloves

2 tsp cumin seeds

2 tsp coriander seeds

2 tsp fennel seeds

2 tsp mustard seeds

2 tsp fenugreek seeds

Whizz all the ingredients together in a spice grinder, and keep in an airtight jar.

Chilli paste

This is a delicious, fiery spice paste, similar to harissa. We use it most regularly for the carrot and green bean salad on page 131, but it is also a great secret weapon to have in your fridge for spicing up pasta, soups, meat and more.

Makes a small jar – keep it in the fridge

1 fairly hot dried chilli (e.g. ancho), rehydrated in hot water for 30 minutes; drained, de-seeded and cut into chunks

1 tbs cumin seeds

1 tbs caraway seeds

25g cayenne

25g sweet paprika

1 good-sized bulb of garlic, cloves separated and peeled

1 tsp salt

75ml sunflower oil

Dry-roast the ground cumin and caraway seeds for a couple of minutes in a small frying pan, until they are beginning to colour and they smell toasty. Allow to cool slightly, then whizz in a spice grinder.

Whizz everything together in a food processor.

Bill's Kitchen
Sweet and savoury salad dressing
Sesame and ginger
Great on noodle and rice salads; gives an Asian twist to crunchy vegetables
Bill's Kitchen
Classic vinaigrette salad dressing
Mustard and dill
Perfect for mixed summer leaves and warm winter salads
250ml℮

Three great dressings

These dressings are so popular in our cafés, we eventually bowed to customer pressure and bottled both the mustard and dill dressing and the sesame and ginger one so you can buy them ready-made. However, if you prefer to make your own, here's how. All these dressings will keep in a cool place for a couple of weeks at least.

They each make about ½ litre

Mustard and dill vinaigrette

30g fresh dill, roughly chopped

2 tbs wholegrain mustard

120ml white wine vinegar

2 tbs runny honey

½ tsp salt

320ml oil (rapeseed or sunflower)

Stuart's classic vinaigrette

2 tbs Dijon mustard

100ml white wine vinegar

½ tsp salt

½ tsp sugar

400ml sunflower oil

Sesame and ginger dressing

35g stem ginger (in syrup)

2 tbs stem ginger syrup

1 tbs sesame seeds

60ml white wine vinegar

80ml soy sauce

320ml oil (rapeseed or sunflower)

Method for all three dressings

Whizz all the ingredients except the oil, either in a food processor, or using a handheld blender. Gradually add the oil whilst still whizzing/blending. Check the seasoning.

Mustard and dill vinaigrette

The mustard and dill is somewhat piquant with a mild grassy/aniseed aroma from the dill. Good for a slightly more sharply dressed green salad and great also with blanched winter vegetables served slightly warm.

Makes about ½ litre. This will keep in a cool place out of the fridge for a couple of weeks at least.

Stuart's classic vinaigrette

This is the classic French dressing, perfect on a fresh round lettuce and any other green salad. Stuart was assured by the French friends who gave him the instructions that the cheapest vegetable oil was all that was required for this – sunflower oil is perfect. Even salt and sugar are embellishments and not essential.

Sesame and ginger dressing

This is probably my favourite dressing, and certainly outsells the mustard and dill by 2 to 1. As well as leafy salads, it's great on noodles and almost anything based on grilled or smoked salmon.

Sweet pastry for tarts

This is the pastry we use in our cafés for all our sweet tarts, and came originally from a French pastry chef I worked with in London. Allow a couple of hours to let it chill thoroughly in the fridge before using. It makes enough for three 23cm tarts, so if that's too much, freeze in clingfilm what you aren't going to use in the next day or so.

200g unsalted butter cubed in 2cm pieces

350g plain white flour

75g caster sugar

2 small eggs, lightly beaten

Whizz the butter and flour together in a food processor, or rub the butter into the flour with the tips of your fingers, lifting the mixture as you do so, until it looks like breadcrumbs. Add the sugar and whizz again, or gently rub the sugar in by hand.

Add the eggs and whizz or hand-mix thoroughly, to gather the crumbs together into a dough. Divide the dough into three equal-sized pieces, cover in clingfilm and chill thoroughly before using.

To blind bake a tart shell pre-heat the oven to 160°C (fan). Roll out the pastry and line your tart tin with it, feeding it gently into the corners of the tin (rather than stretching it). Press it tightly against the sides of the tin and trim it off at the top. On top of the pastry, lay either heat-proof clingfilm (which I use but can be tricky to find) or baking parchment, and then fill the pastry case with baking beans. Put in the oven for 20 minutes, then remove the beans and lining and continue to cook for a further 5-10 minutes until the pastry looks dry but has barely started going golden.

Mince pie pastry

This is an exceptionally delicious and rich pastry, perfect for mince pies, but probably a bit over-the-top for other sweet tarts.

Makes 1kg of pastry, sufficient for about 40 mince pies (see mince pie recipe on page 215).

500g plain flour

½ tsp salt

350g butter, chilled and cubed in 2cm pieces

150g caster sugar

2 egg yolks

2 whole eggs

Whizz flour and salt and chilled butter cubes together in a food processor until the mixture is like breadcrumbs. Add sugar and whizz again very briefly.

Mix egg yolks and whole eggs together. Add to flour mix and pulse a few times until the dough has just come together. Don't overwork it or it will get tough. Divide into two manageable-sized blobs and put in clingfilm. Allow to rest in the fridge for at least an hour before using.

Cream cheese pastry for pies

This pastry is great for all savoury pies. We use it for the beef and ale pie on page 89. And we've recently started making a wild venison and mushroom pie that it's also delicious with. At home we've used it very successfully to make pasties with leftover stew. But if you want a plainer pastry that's also really versatile, try the wholemeal pastry recipe on page 67.

The recipe I give here is also extremely easy to work with.

This quantity is the largest that will fit comfortably into a typical domestic food processor, so if you're making more than one quantity you will probably need to make separate batches of pastry.

For a pie to serve 8 (the kind of pie that only has a lid not a bottom as well)

225g white flour

175g cold butter cubed in 2cm pieces

175g cream cheese

½ tsp salt

Put flour, salt and butter in a food processor and whizz to breadcrumb stage. Add the cream cheese and mix again until it all comes together into a ball.

Chill well – at least 2 hours. Roll out to 7mm thickness; it wants to be a bit thicker than regular shortcrust.

Leftovers: the finest food in the world

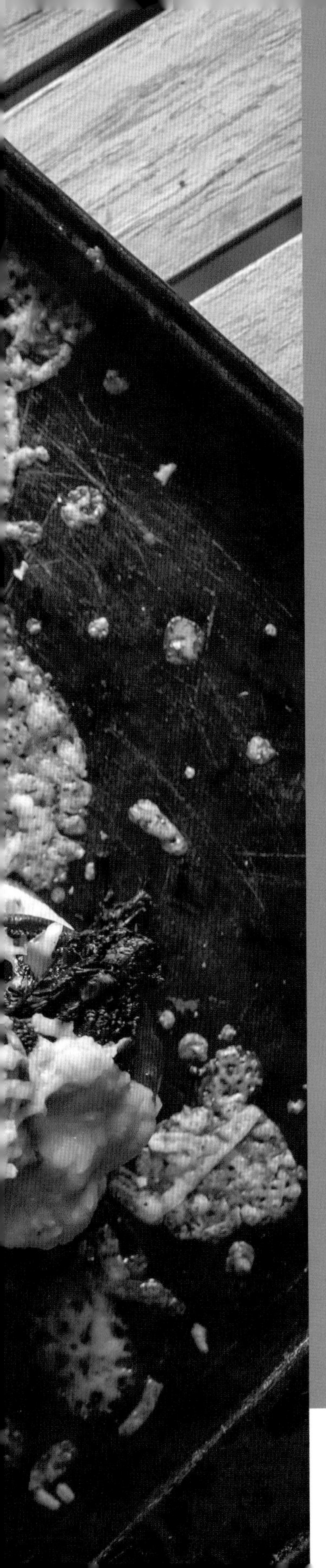

Cooking with leftovers is probably my favourite kind of cooking. I love its creativity and the unexpected and delicious combinations that result. And it appeals to my ever-growing sense of frugality. I hate throwing food away that someone has worked hard to grow or make.

Good leftover cookery is partly about fridge management. If your fridge is crammed full you're likely to miss out on delicious morsels of leftovers which you've stashed behind six pots of yoghurt. The beautiful leftover will shortly become a sad shrivelled-up thing that nobody wants to use. Cooking imaginatively with leftovers is all about using sparkling fresh leftovers before you go shopping again – not about scraping the sides of a dried-up bowl of gloop from the back of the fridge. And whilst I'm hugely in favour of the delicious use of leftovers I don't want anyone to die of food poisoning. If you're in doubt about how many days to keep particular ingredients, there is fail-safe advice on the NHS website.

So, below are some notes on some of the strategies for using leftovers that I've employed during the year it took to write this book (witness the weekday family suppers chapter starting on page 136).

Freezing

Most of this section is about using fresh leftovers. I find that the freezer, like the microwave, is very useful but for a very limited range of purposes. I almost never use it for complete dishes – I'd rather eat Vietnamese beef two nights in a row when it's fresh than have it lurking in the freezer. However, I think the freezer is fantastic for certain foods, such as raw currants and plums, or cooked apple sauce, if you happen to have a glut of fruit in your garden. I also use it to store delicious things I've made too much of, such as tomato sauce (page 241) or meat ragout (such as the brisket recipe on page 229), and of course for ham and chicken stock (pages 225 and 245), after I've cooked the meat. Then there are two really worthwhile frozen vegetables, frozen peas and frozen spinach, and finally I do use it for raw meat, including bacon and sausages, and for bread.

And that's about it.

Using complete dishes

Sometimes complete dishes can be a good starting point for another meal. We've eaten with great pleasure leftover coq au vin (meat stripped from the bones) mixed with roast aubergine and puy lentil casserole (page 107); leftover garlic and mustard chicken (page 79) (chicken stripped from the bones and chopped; potatoes chopped) mixed with curried spinach potato and lentil soup (page 59). Both sensationally good.

Pasties can be good vehicles for leftover casseroles. Either pizza dough or bought puff pastry can contain all kinds of meat and veggie stews, giving them a completely new personality.

I've used spiced pepperonata (page 115) as a relish for cheese sandwiches, and stirred into beef noodles with the addition of some soy sauce and fish sauce.

I often make the roast aubergine ratatouille (page 109) to have with roast lamb. If there's a little lamb and plenty of ratatouille left over, then the next day I chop up the lamb quite small and re-heat it in the ratatouille; at the end I'll add a little crumbled feta and serve the whole thing with either rice or some fresh bread (spianata on page 31 is really good for this).

Potatoes

I always aim to cook more potatoes than I need – especially boiled or baked potatoes.

Some examples:

Fry cut-up boiled potatoes with salt and pepper; towards the end add a little chopped chorizo, then some torn Parma ham; stir in just-boiled runner beans and some lemon juice. Summer deliciousness!

Then there are any number of quick gratins that use leftover cooked potatoes. Add cream or butter, almost any kind of cheese, maybe some tomatoes, maybe some roast peppers, a little ham or bacon, possibly a few anchovies chopped small – and then sprinkle some cheddar or Parmesan on top and bake in a hot oven for 15 minutes. Gourmet leftovers.

And your Spanish omelette or frittata (see page 149) has a head start if you've already got cooked potatoes.

Soup

Soup is perhaps the most obvious and potentially all-encompassing leftover route. But be a little cautious. Blended meat gives soup a slurry-like quality fit only for turkey twizzlers. So take the meat out if you're making a soup from a stew, and chop it finely. Blend the rest of the stew (adding water or stock as necessary), then add back the chopped meat prior to re-heating.

And of course don't forget to use your leftover ham stock (page 225) or your leftover chicken-bone stock (on page 245) – see the soup recipes on page 63.

Salmon & smoked salmon

Leftover salmon or smoked salmon may not feature in your household much but if it does…

Boil some nice new potatoes and toss with leftover cooked salmon or bits of smoked salmon plus some sesame and ginger dressing. Pile on top of some un-dressed but good-quality salad leaves. And you could try adding blanched runner beans. Delicious simplicity.

Chicken

At home we roast the biggest possible chicken with the deliberate aim of creating the maximum amount of leftovers. See page 63 for chicken and sweetcorn soup and page 147 for chicken, leek and lemon risotto.

Additionally leftover roast chicken is utterly lovely for many other things: in noodle stir-fries with garlic, ginger, chillies, soy sauce, fish sauce and sesame oil; in salads or pasta, fried in garlic butter and finished with lemon; in sandwiches with crunchy leaves and (if you're me) Patak's mixed pickle. You'll run out of chicken before you run out of possibilities.

Pork

At home we often cook quite big bits of pork, for instance when making the DIY hog roast. Slow-cooked pork leftovers probably warrant a lot more space, but here are a couple of recent pork-leftover highlights:

I fried some leftover slow-cooked pork shoulder (page 231) in its own fat, with some small cubes of stale white sourdough bread, until the bread was beginning to crisp and the pork was brown in places. I seasoned it well and then mixed it with halved Gardener's Delight tomatoes, some peppery mixed leaves, and mustard and dill dressing (page 249). The resulting warm salad was topped with a few crumbs of Cashel Blue.

A couple of days later I mixed some of the cooked pork with garlic and fennel seeds, Marmande tomatoes, and topped it with semi-mashed Pink Fir Apple potatoes and Montgomery cheddar. Baked in a hot oven for about 20 minutes and served with runner beans - this is leftover cookery at its finest.

Beef

I've found several uses for leftover pulled brisket (page 227); my current favourite is beef crumpets: toasted crumpet, slow-cooked cherry tomatoes, pile of leftover pulled beef, grated cheese. Then put the whole thing in a hot oven for about 15 minutes until the cheese has melted. Beef and cheese sounds a bit weird, but think of it as a sort of cheeseburger 2.0.

Pasta

Re-heating pasta might sound odd, but transforming leftover pasta into a pasta bake can be a pretty satisfactory development. The pasta may not end up al dente but the flavours can be fantastic. And if you also have leftover cooked potatoes, then combining the two carbs together (pasta and potatoes) can also produce great results as long as you add enough stuff that packs a good flavour punch: chorizo, bacon, goats' cheese, sun-dried tomatoes etc. Top it all with some buffalo mozzarella and bake in a hot oven for 20 minutes and you've got a luxurious and quick supper.

Rice

All leftover rice is a gift but the best leftover rice of all is from the spicy chicken and rice recipes on pages 75-77. This is delicious on its own or as an accompaniment to casseroles/curries/stews. Be aware that leftover rice should be refrigerated as soon as possible after cooking, as there are particularly nasty bacteria which can develop in rice left at room temperature, and these particular bacteria are not destroyed even by thorough subsequent re-heating.

Spice mixes and pastes

There are various things that it's easier to make on a larger scale than you're likely to use at a single meal – such as chilli paste (page 247), roast pepper ketchup (page 241) or Ras el Hanout (page 247). Keep them near the front of your fridge/cupboard as reminders. For instance, add some chilli sauce to a tomato sauce for pasta; stir in some roast pepper ketchup to a lentil soup that needs a boost; try a bit of Ras el Hanout on roast lamb.

Chelsea bread & butter pudding.

Chunks of leftover Chelsea buns (page 33) or brioche (pages 37) mixed with blood-orange segments make a delicious pudding when combined with a mixture of 2 beaten eggs and a 250ml pot of cream. It all needs soaking for an hour first, in a medium baking dish – then you sprinkle some demerara sugar on the top and bake in a medium oven for 20 minutes. Utterly yummy.

And with all this leftover cooking, let your imagination and your tastebuds be your guide. Imagine eating the dish that you're creating. Will it taste lovely? Then cook it.

Gardener cook – sort of

Despite living in the depths of the countryside, we are not serious gardeners. Sarah comes from a proper veg-gardening family and has an innate understanding of how it all works, but I have to go to the Gardeners' World website each spring to remind myself how to plant seed potatoes and how to support broad bean plants when they start going floppy. Sarah tends to deal with the greenhouse, which involves skilled work like pinching out the side-shoots of tomatoes (which I've had explained to me several years running and still don't really understand) and I deal more with the outside crops.

However, even the modest amount of veg gardening that we do adds to my cooking. The crops we have success with, and therefore the ones that feature a lot in our summer meals at home, are:

Potatoes: always Charlottes, sometimes Pink Fir Apples and sometimes others

Runner beans: a real discovery for me and now a vegetable I'm happy to eat daily from August to October

Broad beans: to eat when they're young

Courgettes: possibly our most consistently successful crop, much to our Holly and Jonathan's sadness

Tomatoes: Marmande and Gardener's Delight

Cucumbers: the small but smooth-skinned kind

Butternut squash

We also have more sporadic success with sugar snaps, garden peas, sweetcorn and rocket.

And on the fruit side, apart from largely inherited apple and plum trees we only grow rhubarb and blackcurrants. Rhubarb and blackcurrants are particularly wonderful as we don't really do anything to them from one year to the next.

Growing our own veg affects my cooking in two ways.

Firstly I have a feeling of real pride and connection with the food each time I dig up some potatoes or harvest some perky courgettes and ripe tomatoes and make them into a meal straight away. And this pride is all the greater because I can choose to harvest each item at its best point: tomatoes when they're fully ripe; broad beans and runner beans when they're smaller than you'd ever find them in the shops. Courgettes when they're small, shiny and firm.

The second effect on my cooking is that seasonality is a driver of creativity. If you're going to have delicious small fresh runner beans to eat every day for several weeks in a row, then you're likely to find new and delicious things to do with them. So as well as using them in their traditional way as a side vegetable (see 'the best way to cook green vegetables' on page 235), I often use them in salads mixed with tomatoes, crumbly cheeses and fresh herbs, and also in simple pasta dishes.

So as well as saying 'Go forth and cook' I also want to say, 'Go forth and garden – even if you only do it a bit'!

Suppliers & ingredients

Where possible we source our star ingredients from small-scale local producers. This is not a matter of gastronomic political correctness, more a case of following the flavour. Every one of the suppliers listed below provides exceptionally delicious ingredients.

Tudge's bacon, ham, sausages

When my cafés took their first tentative steps away from vegetarianism, inevitably a bacon butty was the first hole in the dyke. It wasn't any old bacon, it was bacon (and then sausages and ham and pork) produced by the Tudge family in North Herefordshire. Gordon Tudge and his sons are passionate believers in producing excellent meat from traditional breeds that live a decent life. A lot of bacon is prepared with smoke flavouring; but at the Tudge's farm each side of bacon is smoked for a week. That's what I call Slow Food.

When we opened in Cambridge we looked for an East Anglian supplier to match the Tudge's quality. However, we're still convinced that what Tudge's offer is unique. So now we export from Herefordshire to Cambridge.

The Tudges are the quintessence of all that is good about local, small scale suppliers: great animal welfare, exceptional flavour and lovely people to deal with. To buy their produce online visit **tudge-meats.co.uk**.

Springfield free-range chickens

Springfield produce delicious and properly free-range chickens just outside Leominster in North Herefordshire. Buy their produce online at **springfieldpoultry.co.uk**

Goats' cheese

We feel proud of the national reputation of the Neal's Yard creamery, whose goats' cheeses, crème fraîche and Greek yoghurt appear daily on the All Saints' menu. Michaelhouse uses the equally delicious and superbly named Wobbly Bottom goats' cheese.

Bread

Increasingly most towns and cities have their own artisan bakeries. All bread is at peak deliciousness when it's fresh, so this is the quintessential food to make ourselves, or to buy from a proper local baker. In Herefordshire, apart from our own All Saints brown bread, you can buy a superb range of breads from Alex Gooch in Hay-on-Wye and Peter Cook, east of Hereford.

Some notes on ingredients

Olive oil: always refers to a basic extra virgin olive oil.

Tomatoes/passata: for tomato-based sauces I use passata at home, but you can equally well use puréed tinned whole tomatoes.

Soy sauce: we use Tamari, which is gluten-free, or Shoyu (cheaper, but not gluten-free).

Butter: salted butter is used for all recipes unless otherwise stated. Add around ½ tsp of salt to a 250g block of butter to go from unsalted to salted butter.

Eggs: medium-size free-range, unless specified otherwise.

Honey: if you have set honey, melt it to make it runny.

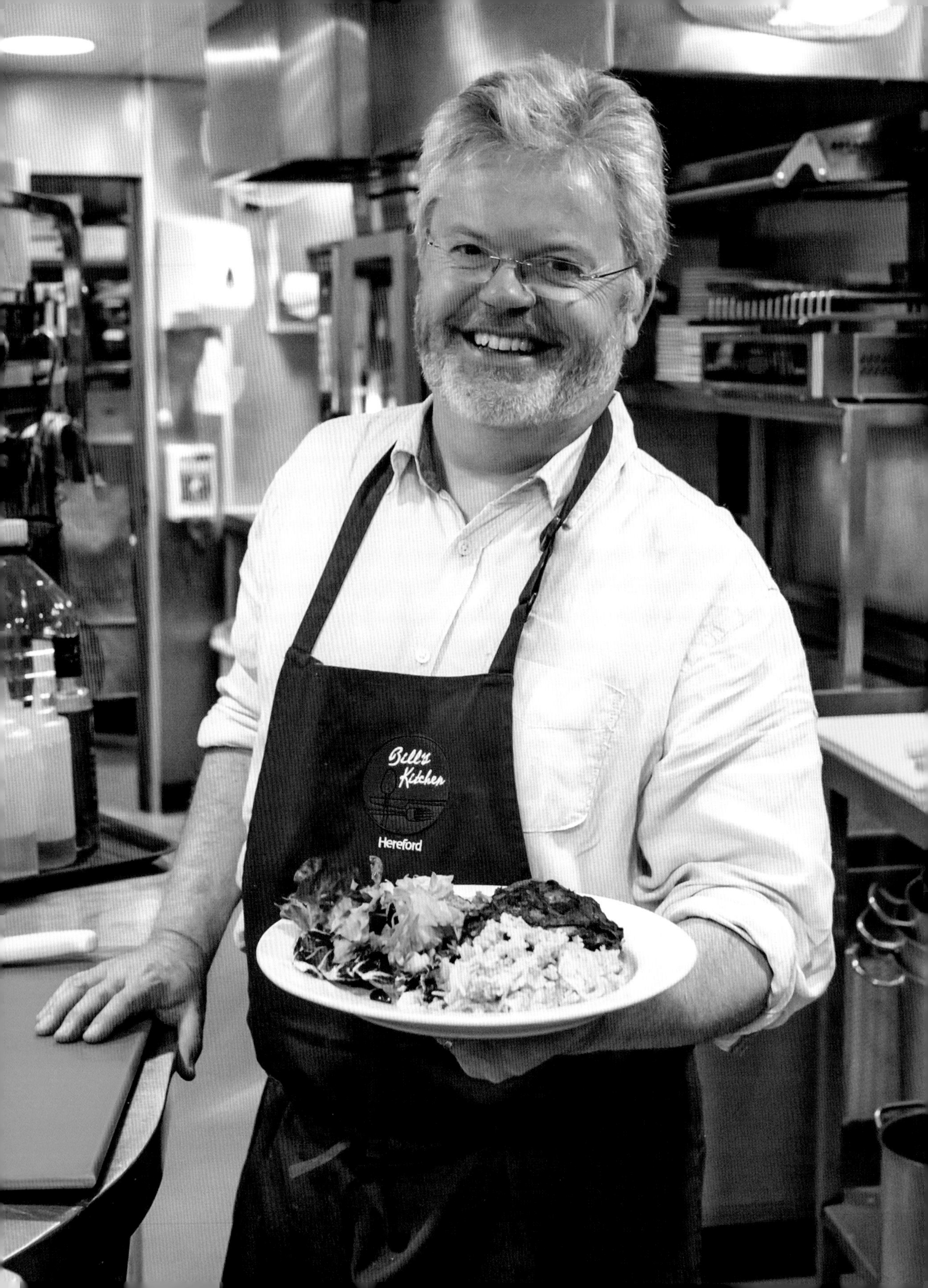
Bill's Kitchen
Hereford

So you'd like to open a café?

It's the same thing that makes five-year old children want to bring their parents very dodgy breakfast in bed on their birthday. There is something deep inside many of us that wants to provide food and wants to get a big smile and a 'thank you' in return. I know from a thousand conversations over the last 30 years that there's a surprisingly large number of people who dream of opening a café, restaurant, tea room or bakery. But if there's any budding café creators reading this book you need to know that failure goes with the territory.

I opened my first café in 1989 and amazingly that café (now called Café Below and no longer under my ownership but still recognizably related to the original 'Place Below') is still alive and well. My two other current kitchens – Café @ All Saints in Hereford and Michaelhouse Café in Cambridge – have been under my direction for a combined total of thirty years. Most catering businesses go bust, so statistically I'm lucky to have survived.

But mine is not a simple story of entrepreneurial endeavour and success. Although three of the cafés I've created have stood (and still stand) the test of time, there have been an equal number of scarring failures. So for any aspiring restaurateurs out there, here's my own list of what are politely called 'learning experiences' – cafés I've created which have not survived under my care – together with some of the lessons I've taken from them. The thing that I would emphasize is that the customers loved all of them but customers loving what you do is not enough for business survival.

The Lemon Tree café in Marylebone

This was a small café, part of a pioneering health centre in the crypt of a large church on the Marylebone Road. I learnt that numbers matter; very cheap premises don't help if the place can't fit in enough customers.

The Refectory at St Davids, Pembrokeshire

A stunningly beautiful modern insertion into a medieval hall, this was attached to the magnificent cathedral. I learnt that however beautiful and large the space, it's hard to make a café work when it is packed during the summer and empty during the winter.

Bill's Café and Deli in Hereford

This was a beautifully designed café just round the corner from All Saints, with half the space given over to a deli. I learnt to stick to what I'm good at. People still talk to me about how much they loved the Deli, but the truth is that although the café part worked really well, the business was never going to work without the deli being really busy too. I discovered that, despite growing up above an antique shop, I'm not a shopkeeper.

So be brave. Follow your dream. Create the most beautiful place. But remember that failure is always possible and make sure that your possible failures are survivable (for more on the delights of failure in life generally, read Tim Harford's excellent *Adapt: Why Success Always Starts with Failure*).

Recipe list

V vegetarian (assuming that vegetarian cheeses are used)

Ve vegan (also vegetarian)

GF gluten-free (assuming that gluten-free mustard, sausages and soy sauce are used and that any accompanying bread or roll is gluten-free)

Bread: daily & less daily

Holiday breakfasts

My favourite soups

Tart or quiche?

Chicken & carbs

Lunch from the café ovens

5 wholesome hotpots

Salads & things to go with them

Weekday family suppers

Friends for dinner

Puddings & tarts

Cakes (& cookies & & traybakes)

Food for feasting

Bits & pieces: relishes, sauces, dressings & pastries

Leftovers: the finest food in the world

Index

D

E

F

G

H

I

J

L

M

N

O

P

Acknowledgements

This book has been an utter pleasure to bring to life, and this is thanks to a lot of work from a large number of people.

Michael Phillips, the wonderful designer of this book, was instrumental in giving me the courage to contemplate a new publication and has had a clear vision from the start of how it should look. Jay Watson has been a joy to work with as well as taking sumptuous photos – and Helen Bricknell kept us clean and organized during the shoots. Marianne Ryan has been a delightful and meticulous editor and Dominic Harbour has brought panache and enthusiasm to the book's promotion and PR.

Thanks also to my wonderful group of recipe testers, whose comments have not only informed individual recipes but also helped me fine-tune my expectations of how the book will be used in practice.

None of it could have happened without the two cafés which not only provide my livelihood but also gave birth to most of the recipes in this book. So huge thanks to the staff team at Café @ All Saints Hereford, led by Dean and Paula, and to the crew at Michaelhouse Café Cambridge, led by Darren and Lownz. And also to Jackie Mumford, an unseen but crucial cog in the café engines.

Recipes never emerge from nowhere and I'm grateful to the myriad sources of knowledge and deliciousness on which I've drawn: to the many wonderful café cooks I've worked with over the years in London, Hereford, Cambridge and St Davids; to friends and family from whom I've mercilessly stolen favourite recipes; and to all the passionate cookery authors who year by year add to the quality of all our eating and cooking lives.

And none of it would be worthwhile without the love and support of my best customers and critics: Sarah, Jonathan and Holly.

First published in Great Britain in 2017 by Archetype Books

A CIP record of this book is available from the British Library.

ISBN 978 1 9997637 0 1

Design
Michael Phillips
archetypedesign.eu

Editing
Marianne Ryan
marianneryan.eu

Photography
Jay Watson
jaywatson.photography

Chris Tudge (page 258)
tudge-meats.co.uk

Print
World Print Ltd
worldprint.com.hk

Archetype Books
Clarendon House
52 Cornmarket Street
Oxford, OX1 3HJ
archetypebooks.net